# Profit-izing

# Your Business

---

## Your Action Plan

### for

### Squeezing the Most

### Out of Everyday Business Activities

---

## Neil Bryan, MBA

Dedication:

To my wife, Maureen.

# Contents:

# PREFACE

Is your business as profitable as possible? How do you know? Do you know what profit is? This book will show you how to measure profit, maintain profit, make the necessary changes to increase profit and keep an eye on all things that can affect profit.

This is not necessarily intended as an accounting primer, but enough accounting concepts will be explained and discussed to give the reader a good foundation for understanding the accounting in his or her business and more importantly, what that accounting means.

I have been involved in the business of installing financial systems, procurement systems and order management and distribution systems for the last thirty years. During that time, I came to realize that the exact same concepts and processes used in these large businesses could be applied to much smaller companies and help those smaller companies thrive. I have an MBA in Finance and forty years of large and small business experience. I have run my own consulting company and worked in accounting and information systems for twenty-five years before that.

I came to understand that many small companies lack knowledge of these processes and/or have the belief that they could not be applied in small companies. But with the proper specific training and knowledge, these concepts and processes can be very useful to any size business.

With this book, I hope to start the process of helping small businesses use what the Big Guys use to measure and control their business and to keep them profitable year after year. As mentioned above, we will concentrate on very specific areas where the most impact can be found.

# INTRODUCTION

The profitability of any company depends on only two things: product and processes.

Because we have no control over what product or service a company sells, the product is secondary in this book but equally important to the bottom line of the company.

In this book we will be itemizing and discussing the processes and controls necessary in each area of the company that can have a significant contribution to the bottom-line profit of the company.

First, let's layout the framework and define exactly what we will be examining in order to help with the organization and management of your business.

Listed below are the processes where the most impact can be made, and these are the ones we will examine in this book. Some of you may recognize the following as accounting applications or other specific areas of your business, but in this book, we will be examining the entire process that surrounds these areas, i.e. not just the specific subject itself.

We will concentrate on the areas where the most action can be taken to help increase your profit and/or reduce your expenses. They are the following.

## Location

The location of your business can play a vital part in your success or failure. We'll provide a checklist to help you determine if your present location or a proposed location for your business meets the needs and is most likely to lead to success.

## Budgeting

We'll look at the whys and how's of budgeting.

# Profit-izing Your Business

## Customer Orders

We'll examine some steps to take to make this activity more efficient and cost effective.

## Accounts Receivable

Three specific techniques for managing, minimizing and profitizing your receivables.

## Accounts Payable

Various methods for profiting from your payables will be discussed and explained.

## Maintaining Inventory

Several inventory management techniques will be examined, and examples will be given of each technique and how it can affect your profits.

# Profit-izing Your Business

## Purchasing

Purchasing refers to the process you use for actually purchasing additional inventory for sale to your customers as well as purchasing other necessary material and equipment for your business.

## Receiving of ordered goods and services

We will look at various methods and things to consider for this activity to minimize any negative impact on profits.

## The Daily Action Plan

What should you do daily to ensure that your business is running smoothly and more importantly that it is maximizing the profit potential for the business? We'll define a checklist that you should actively use on a daily basis for this purpose.

# Profit-izing Your Business

## The Monthly Action Plan

As with the daily plan, there are actions you should take on a monthly basis to check on the health of your business. We'll define a plan and a checklist for this monthly activity.

## Payroll

We'll suggest some ways to minimize payroll costs and time and also put some control in the payroll process itself.

## Petty Cash

We'll look at the what petty cash is for, whether you really need it, how to eliminate it, and if you really need it, how to control and manage it.

# Profit-izing Your Business

## Loans to Employees

In this chapter, we'll look at the various reasons for and against this practice, how to handle the loan process and how to profit from this activity.

## Loans to Self

We'll examine this practice and list the pros and cons. We'll also suggest how to do this and not impact the business profitability.

## Marketing and Advertising

We'll define the difference between advertising and marketing and  take a look at the various methods of advertising and marketing.

# Profit-izing Your Business

## Computer systems

All businesses can benefit from the proper computer system that will help control the various aspects of the business. We won't get into recommending specific software but will give you enough so you can select your own with some degree of confidence.

## Controls

Some small businesses don't concern themselves with any controls over the processes within the company because they consider themselves too small to worry about it. However, lack of proper controls can lead to employees and customers taking advantage of the situation and costing you money. We'll look at the controls that large companies put in place and how they can be used in smaller businesses. Most forms of control will be mentioned in the individual chapters but here we will discuss others that you may want to consider.

## Your Employees

Always remember your employees are the heart of your business. Employee benefits are a crucial aspect of any company's strategy to retain its employees. We'll look at some employee retention processes to help you maintain a trained and knowledgeable staff.

## Summary

After studying this book and putting the various procedures into practice, you will, at the very least, feel more organized in your business affairs and eventually will see some increase in your annual profit percentage. We don't guarantee the success of every business simply by applying these techniques – no one could do that. There are too many variables in the business world to guarantee anything. But we do feel strongly that applying these techniques to your business will significantly improve the organization and management of your business and lay the

# Profit-izing Your Business

groundwork for improved profits either through greater revenue or lower costs.

# Profit-izing Your Business

# BUDGETING for PROFIT

## Why prepare a budget?

There are several reasons why a company should prepare a budget:

Planning: A budget helps a company plan its financial activities and allocate resources effectively. It enables management to set financial goals and objectives and identify the resources necessary to achieve them. A budget helps to ensure that the company has adequate cash flow to meet its obligations and invest in growth opportunities.

Control: A budget provides a framework for monitoring and controlling financial activities. It allows management to compare actual results with budgeted amounts and identify variances that require corrective action. By tracking actual performance against the budget, management can identify potential problems early and take corrective action to avoid financial difficulties.

Decision-making: A budget provides information for decision-making. It helps management to evaluate alternative courses of action and make informed decisions about investing in new projects or activities. A budget can also help management to evaluate the financial impact of changes in the business environment or changes in strategy.

Communication: A budget provides a means of communication between different levels of management and between management and stakeholders such as shareholders, creditors, and investors. It helps to ensure that everyone has a common understanding of the company's financial goals and objectives.

# Profit-izing Your Business

Motivation: A budget can be used as a motivational tool to encourage employees to achieve financial targets. It provides a clear set of goals and objectives that employees can work towards, and it can be used to reward performance that exceeds budgeted targets.

Overall, preparing a budget is a fundamental aspect of financial management for any company. It provides a framework for planning, control, decision-making, communication, and motivation, and is essential for achieving financial success.

## What's included in a business budget?

A business budget is a financial plan that outlines how much money a business expects to receive and spend over a specific period, usually a year. A budget typically includes the following elements:

# Profit-izing Your Business

Revenue projections: This includes estimates of how much money the business expects to earn from sales, services, or other sources.

Expense projections: This includes estimates of how much the business expects to spend on items such as salaries, rent, utilities, marketing, and other costs associated with running the business.

Capital expenditures: This includes any large investments the business plans to make during the budget period, such as purchasing new equipment or expanding to a new location.

Cash flow projections: This projection outlines how much cash the business expects to have on hand at the end of each month, based on its revenue and expense projections.

# Profit-izing Your Business

Contingency plan: This plan outlines how the business will handle unexpected events, such as a sudden drop in sales or a major expense that was not accounted for in the original budget.

A well-designed business budget should be detailed, realistic, and flexible enough to accommodate changes in the business environment. Regularly tracking and comparing actual results to the budget is also important to ensure that the business is on track to meet its financial goals.

What does a budget to actual report look like?

A budget to actual report is a financial report that compares the budgeted amounts to the actual amounts spent or earned during a particular period of time. The report typically includes the following components:

# Profit-izing Your Business

Budgeted amounts: This section outlines the original budgeted amounts for revenue, expenses, and other financial metrics for the period in question.

Actual amounts: This section outlines the actual amounts spent or earned for revenue, expenses, and other financial metrics for the period in question.

Variance analysis: This section compares the budgeted amounts to the actual amounts and calculates the variance (the difference between the two). The variance is typically expressed both in absolute dollar amounts and as a percentage of the budgeted amount. Positive variances indicate that actual amounts were higher than budgeted amounts, while negative variances indicate that actual amounts were lower than budgeted amounts.

Explanation of variances: This section provides an explanation for the variances, highlighting the reasons why actual amounts differed from budgeted amounts. This may include explanations for both positive and negative variances.

Recommendations for future periods: Based on the analysis of variances, this section may provide recommendations for future periods, such as adjustments to the budget, changes to spending or revenue generation practices, or other financial strategies.

Overall, the purpose of the Budget to Actual Report is to provide an accurate and objective analysis of an organization's financial performance, and to identify areas for improvement or optimization.

## Budgeting Techniques

There are several different budgeting techniques that companies can use. Here are some examples:

# Profit-izing Your Business

Incremental budgeting: This technique involves using the previous year's budget as a starting point and making adjustments for changes in the business environment or the company's strategic objectives.

Zero-based budgeting: This technique involves starting from scratch each year and building the budget from the ground up. All expenses must be justified, and no assumptions are made about the previous year's spending.

Activity-based budgeting: This technique involves identifying the activities that drive costs in the organization and building the budget around those activities. This can help to ensure that resources are allocated to the activities that provide the most value to the organization.

# Profit-izing Your Business

Rolling budgeting: This technique involves creating a budget that covers a set period of time, such as a year, and then updating it on a rolling basis as the year progresses. This allows the company to adjust the budget based on actual results and changes in the business environment.

Flexible budgeting: This technique involves creating a budget that can be adjusted based on changes in volume or other factors. This can help to ensure that the budget remains relevant and accurate even as business conditions change.

Top-down budgeting: This technique involves setting overall financial targets for the company and then allocating resources to different departments or business units based on those targets.

# Profit-izing Your Business

Bottom-up budgeting: This technique involves involving employees at all levels of the organization in the budgeting process. Employees are asked to provide input on their department's needs and priorities, and this input is used to build the budget from the bottom up.

Each budgeting technique has its own advantages and disadvantages, and the choice of technique will depend on the specific needs and circumstances of the organization.

Regardless of what method you use on an annual basis, the Zero-based budgeting technique (sometimes combined with Bottom-up budgeting) should be used every three to five years to force yourself to examine closely your income and expenses.

For expediency each year, another method can be used for most years.

# Profit-izing Your Business

When you examine your Budget to Actual Report and find many large variances, it may be time to use Zero-based budgeting even though it is the most time-consuming technique.

# Profit-izing Your Business

# DESIGNING YOUR ACCOUNTING FOR EASY TAX PREPARATION

To make your annual tax preparation easier, here are some tips for organizing your accounting.

1. If you live and/or pay business taxes in the United States, base your accounting categories and accounts on the Income, Expenses and Cost of Goods Sold Sections of the IRS Schedule C form.

2. Don't try to include too much detail into your expense accounts by defining one for each individual type of expense. Some expenses can be grouped with no loss of information and an easier tax time.

3. If you have vehicles as part of your business, also review the Information on Your Vehicle Section before you define your accounts.

# Profit-izing Your Business

4.  Review the Schedule C each year to see if you need to make any changes to your accounting.

# CUSTOMER ORDERS – THE BASICS

## FUNDAMENTALS OF CUSTOMER SERVICE

Where would the company be without orders from your customers? This is where it all begins; without customer orders there is no company. So, what can a company do with customer orders that can positively affect the profitability of the company?

Customer service is the provision of assistance and support to customers before, during, and after a purchase. Here are some fundamental principles of customer service:

Understanding the Customer:

Understanding the needs, wants, and expectations of the customer is the first step in providing quality customer service.

# Profit-izing Your Business

### Active Listening:

Active listening is a critical skill for customer service representatives. It involves paying attention to the customer, understanding their concerns, and providing appropriate solutions.

### Empathy:

Empathy involves putting yourself in the customer's shoes and understanding their perspective. It helps you to connect with the customer and provide a more personalized experience.

### Communication:

Effective communication is essential for providing quality customer service. Clear, concise, and professional communication helps to build trust and establish a good rapport with the customer.

Timeliness:

Timeliness is important in customer service. Responding to customer inquiries and complaints promptly shows that you value their time and are committed to resolving their issues.

Problem-solving:

Effective problem-solving is a crucial part of customer service. It involves identifying the root cause of the problem and finding an appropriate solution that satisfies the customer.

Continuous Improvement:

Continuous improvement involves regularly evaluating and improving the customer service process to ensure that it meets the changing needs and expectations of the customers.

In summary, providing quality customer service involves understanding the customer, active listening, empathy, effective communication, timeliness, problem-solving, and continuous improvement.

## Ensuring accuracy in customer orders

Ensuring accuracy in customer orders is crucial for providing good customer service and building a strong reputation for your business. Here are some steps you can take to help ensure order accuracy:

Train your staff: Make sure your staff is trained to take accurate orders. They should be familiar with the menu and any special requests or modifications that customers may make.

Repeat the order: Have your staff repeat the order back to the customer to confirm that it is correct. This can help catch any mistakes or misunderstandings before the order is processed.

# Profit-izing Your Business

Use order tracking software: Consider using software to track orders and ensure they are fulfilled accurately. This can help prevent mistakes and provide a record of what was ordered.

Clarify any special requests: If a customer makes a special request or modification to their order, make sure to clarify exactly what they want. This can help prevent misunderstandings and ensure the order is fulfilled correctly.

Double-check the order: Before sending out the order, double-check it to make sure everything is correct. This can help catch any mistakes or oversights.

Follow up with the customer: After the order has been delivered, follow up with the customer to make sure everything was correct and to address any concerns they may have. This can help build customer loyalty and prevent future issues.

# Profit-izing Your Business

By taking these steps, you can help ensure that customer orders are accurate and minimize the risk of errors or misunderstandings.

## The Customer Order Process

Before examining the customer order process and possible actions to take, let's look at what kind of orders we're talking about. Depending on the type of company you are, your customer orders may be different.

Customer Order Types:

Direct Orders

For companies with only retail locations, the orders are all "over the counter" usually including immediate payment either in cash or by credit card. In some cases, however, even these types of orders are allowed to "run a tab" and get billed monthly for their purchases.

# Profit-izing Your Business

### Phone Orders

Customer orders taken over the phone are another type of direct order and are usually treated in much the same way, with payment by debit or credit card at the time of the order. However, just as with "over the counter" orders, there are times when customers calling in phone orders are allowed to accumulate these orders and receive a bill at end of the month for all the purchases they made.

### Internet Orders

For companies with only an internet presence, your customer orders are usually generated by the customer by selecting the items they wish to purchase and putting in the information for delivery address and payment information. Usually, in this instance, the payment is by credit or debit card so you, as the business owner, don't need to concern yourself with collecting the payment.

# Profit-izing Your Business

## Professional Service Customer Orders

There are also companies for which a customer order is a very different document, i.e. professional service firms such as attorneys, accountants, consultants, architects, etc. These types of firms usually have a customer order in the form of a contract for services, usually specifying a total dollar amount, a number of hours, a specific time period or any combination of the three. These may also require a monthly or annual retainer fee to maintain the services.

Now that you've read through the descriptions above, we need to simplify what we are talking about. You've probably been questioning what exactly constitutes a customer order in your own business based on the above descriptions. If someone comes into your business and buys a candy bar, you most definitely don't need to gather any kind of information about that customer. All you need to know for your business purposes is that it was a cash or credit card sale so the proper actions can be taken to account for that sale. So, here is the definition of exactly what we are talking about when we say "Customer Orders".

---

**Definition of Customer Orders** (as discussed in this book):

Customer orders are those purchases from your company that result in the creation of an accounts receivable balance OR will require shipping / delivery of items or services at a later date OR will require you to bill the customer in the future for the purchases.

---

Notice that the above definition specifically excludes over the counter cash purchases and purchases by credit card where the customer is taking the item with them at the time of purchase. But, let me say one thing about over the counter cash purposes. There should always be a receipt generated for the purchase even if it is only a candy bar and even if the customer doesn't want or need the receipt. You will need these receipts or at least a total of them for balancing out your cash register.

With that in mind, let's analyze what can be done with customer orders that could have a significant impact on your profitability.

First, let's examine the contents of a customer order.

## Contents of a Customer Order:

Contents of a Customer Order:

There are certain items of information that must be included in a customer order no matter how you take the order. These items are essential for defining the order and for your company to know what to do with the order itself. These items of information are:

# Profit-izing Your Business

There are certain items of information that must be included in a customer order no matter how you take the order. These items are essential for defining the order and for your company to know what to do with the order itself. These items of information are:

1. Customer Order Number / Invoice Number

2. Complete customer name

3. Complete customer billing address

4. Complete customer delivery address if different from above

5. Contact person at the company

6. Contact phone number

7. Contact email if they have one

8. Contact FAX if they have one

9. Payment Term (if not Cash, Credit/Debit Card or a Professional Service Contract)

    a. Payment terms will be discussed more fully in the Chapter on Accounts Receivable.

# Profit-izing Your Business

10.Payment terms:

    a.  Cash payment at time of order

    b.  Credit card – get credit card number and expiration date

    c.  Debit card – get debit card number

    d.  On Account – this refers to those customers who maintain accounts with you and pay after being billed monthly. (include your internal customer account number on order)

    e.  Based on Service or Hours – this refers to those customers who pay you based on your performance of a particular service or for approved hours spent on the contract.

    f.  Down payment with order and balance in a certain number of payments, days, weeks, months, etc.

11.Complete details of the items being purchased or the service to be performed.

a. For items being purchased, a complete description of the item, the quantity being purchased and the extended amount

b. For Services, a detailed description of what service is to be performed, the time period, the hourly rate (if applicable).

So, with that general definition of customer orders, let's analyze each customer order type and present some specific examples of how to improve in this area.

## Direct Orders - Over the Counter or by Phone

When you take a direct order (other than an over-the-counter cash order), either in person or by phone, how do you do it and what do you do with it?

Here's what should happen.

# Profit-izing Your Business

1. Take the order on a predefined order form that requires all the necessary spaces to be completed by the order taker.

2. Give a copy to your Customer for review and give them a signed copy either in person or by mail or email. If this is an in-person order, the Customer should also be asked to review and sign the order indicating acceptance before it is finalized. This is especially true if you are dealing with larger dollar amounts (by your definition)

3. If the order will require additional payments, send a copy to your Accounts Receivable Department or person to be sure the customer will be billed for any addition amount they owe.

4. Send a copy to your Shipping Department or person to make sure the shipment is handled.

5. File the Original in your Monthly Sales Folder (if you aren't using a computerized order system).

## Internet Orders

When you take an Internet order how do you do it and what do you do with it?

Here's what should happen.

1. The Customer should be provided with an Order Form that requires all the necessary information for fulfilling the order.

2. The Order Form should calculate any tax and shipping charges required. You may want to provide the customer with a selection of shipping options for their selection; Standard, Expedited, Overnight, etc.

3. When the order is complete, provide a copy to your Customer by mail or by email.

4. If the Order will require additional payments, send a copy to your Accounts Receivable Department or person to be sure the customer will be billed for any addition amount they owe.

# Profit-izing Your Business

5. Send a copy to your Shipping Department or Service Department or person to make sure the shipment or service is handled.

6. File the Original in your Monthly Sales Folder (if you aren't using a computerized order system).

## Professional Service Customer Orders

When you take a Professional Service Order how do you do it and what do you do with it?

Here's what should happen.

1. Take the order on a predefined order form that requires all the necessary spaces to be completed by the order taker. In the case of professional services, this can also be a contract for services that both the Customer and the Service Provider sign and date.

2. Give a copy to your Customer for review and send them a signed copy either by mail or email. If this is an in-person order, the Customer should also be asked to

review and sign the order indicating acceptance before it is finalized. This is especially true if you are dealing with larger dollar amounts (by your definition)

3. Send a copy to your Accounts Receivable Department or person to be sure the customer will be billed for any addition amount they owe.

4. Send a copy to your Service Department or the person who will provide the service to make sure the service is handled.

5. File the Original in your Monthly Sales Folder (if you aren't using a computerized order system).

This is a summary of the action that should be taken with each order.

➤ Customer Orders should be in writing (meaning in hard copy format, not necessarily handwritten).

➤ The Customer Order should contain all the detail needed to avoid any mistakes in shipping or delivery of the services.

- ➤ The customer should receive a copy of the order and agree to the details of the order.
- ➤ If payment was not received with the order, a copy of the order must be provided to your accounts receivable department?
- ➤ Your Shipping or Service Delivery Department must receive a copy of the order?

## Some additional detail about Customer Orders.

### ARE MY CUSTOMER ORDERS IN WRITING?

This may seem rather silly at first glance. But, based on my experience, many companies take orders over the phone and simply scribble the information on a sheet of paper and hand it over to someone to fill the order. While this may seem like a very efficient process, let's discuss the problems that may occur.

Handwriting is inherently a very unreliable method for taking orders because of the possibility of not being able to read it after the fact. This leads to errors in shipping, either in quantity or the actual item shipped, errors in pricing and numerous hours spent fixing the errors.

So, what can you do to alleviate this possible problem? The best way is to have a computerized system for taking orders. But, if the company hasn't gotten to that yet, there are other ways. First, have a specific order form that leads the order taker through the steps and information needed to fulfill the order. Second, have a method of verifying the order (read the significant information back to the customer for their approval, print (or make) a copy of the order for the customer to review and sign).

# Profit-izing Your Business

What to do

Customer Orders – in writing, sequentially numbered or computerized, provide copy to customer and to person responsible for the receivables, be detailed about what was ordered or purchased,

How does this have to do with profitability?

By putting more control in the customer order process, you can avoid problems that may occur such as incorrect shipments, incorrect pricing, etc and also avoid the time and expenses of correcting these issues. This will have an impact on the opinion of your customers when it comes to doing business with you.

About Correcting Errors

If you do make an error in shipping or pricing or some other area, the best approach for your business is to admit your error and take any action necessary to correct the error. Your error should not cost the customer either in time arguing about the error or in additional expenses of shipping, returning incorrect items, etc.

# ENERGIZING YOUR ACCOUNTS RECEIVABLE

What do we mean by Accounts Receivable?

| **Accounts Receivables defined** |
|---|
| Simply stated, its money owed to you from your customers as a result of your sales of items or services to the customer. The key is that the customer owes you money. If the money was collected at the time of the sale or performance of the service, it is not part of your accounts receivable balance. |

Remember, when you allow a customer to buy from you and agree to bill them and receive payment later, you are, in effect, lending that customer your money.

REMEMBER, A CUSTOMER ACCOUNTS RECEIVABLE BALANCE IS A LOAN FROM YOU TO THE CUSTOMER.

When you're looking at your accounts receivable, there are four questions to keep in mind:

Are my accounts receivables under control?

What can I do to reduce my accounts receivable and get them under control?

Should I charge a finance charge for past due accounts receivable payments?

What steps do I need to take on past due receivable balances?

These are the questions we will answer in this chapter. So, let's take these questions individually and provide some insight.

**Are my accounts receivables under control?**

What do we mean by under control?

# Profit-izing Your Business

The first action in determining the answer to this is to prepare an accounts receivable aging. An aging is simply a list of all your accounts receivable by customer name, the total amount each customer owes you and then a columnar listing of how much of the customer's balance is current by your terms (due within 30 days, for example), and how much is past due, usually in three other categories; 30 to 60 days past due, 60 to 90 days past due and over 90 days past due.

An analysis of this report will determine if your accounts receivable is under control.

Let's consider some examples:

Review the following Accounts Receivable Aging Report:

# Profit-izing Your Business

| Sample Company | Accounts Receivable Aging | | | As of Date 28-Feb-23 | |
|---|---|---|---|---|---|
| Customer | Total Balance | Current Balance | 30 to 60 Days Past Due | 60 to 90 Days Past Due | Over 90 Days Past Due |
| Acme Computers | 5000 | 4000 | 500 | 500 | |
| Beta Software | 5000 | 4500 | 500 | | |
| Dell Computers | 5000 | 5000 | | | |
| Down & Out, LLP | 5000 | 1500 | 1000 | 1500 | 1000 |
| I Don't Pay, Inc | 5000 | | | | 5000 |
| Office Supplies Store | 5000 | 4500 | 250 | 250 | |
| Microsoft Software | 5000 | 5000 | | | |
| | | | | | |
| Totals | 35000 | 24500 | 2250 | 2250 | 6000 |
| Percent | 100 | 70.00% | 6.43% | 6.43% | 17.14% |
| Ideal Goal | | 100.00% | 0% | 0% | 0% |
| Acceptable Goal | | 95.00% | 2.00% | 2.00% | 1.00% |

Assume this is all your accounts receivable for the purposes of this discussion. First, look at the percent row. This indicates the percentage of each column as compared to the total of all your accounts receivable, i.e. your current balance of $24,500 is 70% of your total accounts receivable, your Over 30 to 60 Days Past Due balance of $2,250 is 6.4% of the total, etc. Now, consider this. If none of the past due balances were ever paid, would it hurt your business? You bet it would! Why? Because you have already sold these customers your goods or services and, unless what you sold can be repossessed, you are out that amount of money.

Now, look at the Goal rows. Of course, the Ideal Goal is to have all your receivables balances current and paying on time. That's very seldom the case but congratulations if it is for you. The Acceptable Goals are what you should be working toward to consider your receivables under control. These percentages represent where your receivables should be as far as percent in each column: i.e. Current should be **95% or greater**, 30 to 60 should be **2% or less, etc**

**What can I do to reduce my accounts receivable balances?**

Review your Accounts Receivable Aging and take some action.

# Profit-izing Your Business

Looking at the Aging Report above, there are some immediate actions you can take to start to get your receivables under control. Take the case of your worst unpaid balances, Down & Out, LLP and Don't Pay, Inc. You should immediately consider whether you should be selling to them at all. In the case of Don't Pay, Inc, the aging indicates that you have stopped selling to them, they have started buying from someone else or they are out of business. After contacting them (or trying to), you should probably take immediate legal action either way to collect what's owed to you and put them on your Do Not Sell To list.

The case of Down & Out, LLP is a little different. Because there are totals in each column, you have apparently been selling to them on a regular basis. If you made a conscious decision to do this and you have reason to believe they will eventually pay the entire balance, go ahead and continue selling to them. Otherwise, you should probably stop selling to them at least until they bring their account current or make some significant payment.

Other customer accounts on this sample aging are not so clear cut. Acme Computers and Office Supplies Store each have a large current balance but also have some 30 to 60 and some 60 to 90 past due amounts. These are customers you definitely want to call and find out what the problem may be. Sometimes an oversight or a lost document can be the answer and they can bring the account up to date. An account can always be put on temporary hold (meaning no more purchases until a significant payment is received).

# Profit-izing Your Business

### Establish a Do Not Sell To List

I mentioned above a Do Not Sell To List. Every company should have one based in part on this review of your receivables. Otherwise, you are continuing to sell to someone who may never pay for your goods or services.

### Establish a Watch List

In the example above, Acme Computers and Office Supply Store should be on your watch list. This list should include those customers that you have contacted for payment so that you can monitor the progress daily.

### Offer a Discount for Cash Payments

Another technique used to reduce receivables is to offer a discount for cash payments. This can be any percentage that you can afford based on your profit margin (this is the difference between the purchase price of the item and your sales price)

### Accept Credit and Debit Cards for Payment

# Profit-izing Your Business

Credit and Debit card payments could be considered the same as cash except for the fees charged for credit card use. Either way, you get you money immediately and don't have to worry about collecting at a later date.

Offer a discount for early payment.

You may be familiar with this but if you aren't, here's how it works. On your invoices you indicate Payment Terms so that the customer knows that you are offering a discount for certain terms. As an example, Payment Terms of 2% 10, Net 30 are very common terms. This means that if the customer pays within 10 days from the invoice date, they can reduce their payment by 2% and you will accept the payment as payment in full for that invoice. Otherwise, the full balance is due within 30 days. You are free to define your own payment terms. Be sure to include them on your customer orders / invoices so that your customers know about them. The larger the discount you offer, the more likely your customers will take advantage of it.

# Profit-izing Your Business

*Note:* Offering a significant discount and keeping track of which customers do not take the discount can give you a heads up as to which customers may be having trouble and maybe should be on your Watch List.

## Should I charge a finance charge for past due accounts receivable payments?

Always remember, your receivables really represent loan balances. You have temporarily lent your customer money to buy your product or services. Ask yourself, "How long do I want to lend this customer my money to allow them to buy from me without charging them"?

Normally, if a customer pays within the terms established by you (usually within 30 days), there is no charge for this. When payments are later than that is when the issue comes into play. Should you charge a finance charge? The answer to this is not as easy as you might expect.

# Profit-izing Your Business

You can charge some customers and not charge others but to do this you must have very specific and defined rules. These rules have to specify under what conditions the customer will be charged, for example, all balances over 30 days past due if the customer has had other past due balances OR all customers with balances over 30 days past due, etc.

The common past due charge is 1 percent per month but you can establish any finance charge as long as it doesn't exceed the federal and state usury laws. These laws change frequently so before you start charging, find out what the legal maximum annual rate is where you do business, so you don't get yourself in trouble by charging too much.

A finance charge should be a gentle reminder to the customer that you have lent them money but you are not in the business of long term loans so you would like payment on the unpaid balance.

Also, keep in mind that you will never see a credit card company not charging interest on the unpaid balance after 30 days. So, why should you be any different?

### Accounts Receivable Tickler

If you are using a manual system, an easy way to keep track of projected payment receipts from your customers is to set up a 31-day tickler system. As you sell something that the customer will pay for later, file a copy of the customer order / invoice in the day corresponding to the day you expect payment. As each day arrives, review what's in the file and determine if the invoices have been paid. This can serve as another control method for maintaining your accounts receivable.

In a computerized system, the system will keep track of what is owed to you and the date each invoice is due. A list of past due customer payments can then be printed, and the appropriate action taken.

Profit-izing Your Business

## How do you control your accounts receivable?

Managing accounts receivable is essential for any business that sells goods or services on credit. Here are the steps to take to control your accounts receivable:

Establish clear payment terms:

Setting clear payment terms at the beginning of the transaction helps to avoid confusion and disputes about when payment is due. This includes specifying the payment due date, any late payment fees or interest charges, and the acceptable methods of payment.

Screen your customers:

Screening your customers helps to minimize the risk of non-payment. Before extending credit, it's important to check the credit history and financial stability of your customers. You can use credit reports, trade references, and other tools to assess the creditworthiness of potential customers.

# Profit-izing Your Business

Invoice promptly:

Sending invoices promptly and accurately is crucial to ensure timely payment. Invoices should include a detailed description of the products or services provided, the amount owed, and any payment terms. By sending invoices promptly, you ensure that your customers have all the information they need to make payment on time.

Follow up on late payments:

Following up on late payments is important to ensure that you get paid as soon as possible. You can use automated reminders, phone calls, or collections agencies to follow up on late payments. By staying on top of late payments, you can prevent them from becoming uncollectible debts.

Offer incentives for early payment:

Offering incentives for early payment can encourage customers to pay on time or even ahead of schedule. This can include discounts, freebies, or other benefits that provide value to the customer while also helping you to get paid faster.

Monitor accounts receivable:

Monitoring your accounts receivable on a regular basis helps you to identify any issues or trends. You can use tools like aging reports and cash flow projections to keep track of outstanding invoices and predict future cash flow. By staying on top of your accounts receivable, you can take action to address any issues before they become problematic.

Review your credit policies:

Regularly reviewing your credit policies helps you to stay up-to-date with industry best practices and ensure that your policies are effective. You can use feedback from customers, industry benchmarks, and other data to fine-tune your credit policies and improve your overall cash flow management.

By following these steps, you can control your accounts receivable and improve your cash flow management. This will help you to maintain a healthy financial position and grow your business over the long term.

# PROFITING FROM ACCOUNTS PAYABLE

What do we mean by Accounts Payable?

| **Accounts Payable defined** |
| --- |
| Simply stated, this is money you owe to someone else as a result of your purchases of products for sale in your company or for other items such as supplies, office furniture and equipment. The key is that you owe money to someone. If you purchased something and paid cash or by credit card, that purchase is not part of your Accounts Payable. |

What can be done with Accounts Payable that will affect your profitability in a positive way?

Ask yourself these questions.

Do I pay my bills on time or early every month?

Can I postpone purchases to delay any cash outlay?

Can I get a better deal on purchases by shopping around or getting bids?

Let's discuss these questions in detail one at a time.

## Do I pay my bills on time or early every month?

You may immediately say yes to this but, as the business owner, you should do some more work to determine this.

### Accounts Payable Analysis

First, periodically prepare an Accounts Payable Analysis. This is not necessarily a monthly report but should be done at least every six months. This is similar to the Accounts Receivable Aging report you prepared for your receivables. This report should list all the suppliers that you *paid* money to, the date and amount you paid. If you have a large number of paid invoices for the month selected for analysis, just select a sample of payments that will represent your total payments. Be sure to select payments made to your major suppliers as part of that sample. Then look up on the paid invoice the due date of what was paid taking into account any terms offered by the supplier. This can be prepared on a spreadsheet by hand or on a computer spreadsheet. Refer to the sample below for the format to use. This may be a time-consuming exercise but can also be very enlightening.

**Review the following Accounts Payable Analysis Report.**

# Profit-izing Your Business

## Accounts Payable Analysis Report

**Sample Company**

**As of Date 28-Feb-23**

| Customer | Amount Paid | Invoice Number | Invoice Amount | Date Paid | Invoice Date | Terms Date for Discount | Terms Date for Full Pay | Discount Percent | Discount Amount if paid on Discount Date | Discount Taken |
|---|---|---|---|---|---|---|---|---|---|---|
| ABC Supply Co | $1,400 | 1237 | $1,400 | 10-Feb | 8-Feb | 18-Feb | 10-Mar | 2.00% | $28.00 | N |
|  | $800 | 1346 | $800 | 10-Feb | 21-Jan | 31-Jan | 20-Feb | 2.00% | $16.00 | N |
| Acme Computers | $600 | 791 | $600 | 10-Feb | 1-Feb | 11-Feb | 3-Mar | 3.00% | $18.00 | N |
| Furniture Company | $2,300 | 235 | $2,300 | 17-Feb | 12-Jan | 22-Jan | 11-Feb | 2.00% | $46.00 | N |
| Office Supply Store | $1,100 | 133 | $1,100 | 17-Feb | 27-Jan | 6-Feb | 26-Feb | 5.00% | $55.00 | N |
| Product Company | $10,300 | 555 | $10,300 | 17-Feb | 10-Feb | 20-Feb | 12-Mar | 2.00% | $206.00 | N |
| XYZ Supply Co | $5,800 | 743 | $5,800 | 17-Feb | 8-Feb | 18-Feb | 10-Mar | 3.00% | $174.00 | N |
| Total Payments | $22,300 |  |  |  |  |  |  |  |  |  |
| Total Savings from Discounts if taken |  |  |  |  |  |  |  |  | $543.00 |  |
| Percent of Savings |  |  |  |  |  |  |  |  | 2.43% |  |

# Profit-izing Your Business

Assume that this report represents all of the payments you made during the month, or a carefully selected sample as explained above.  Also, for the purposes of this report, we assumed that all the invoices were fully due in 30 days, but we assigned different discount percentages to some for illustration purposes. We also assumed that all discounts were for paying within 10 days of the invoice date.

With those criteria in mind, let's review the information in the report.

### ABC Supply Co

ABC Supply was paid for 2 invoices during the month. Each invoice was paid at the full amount of the invoice on Feb 10. The Invoice dates indicate that one invoice was dated Feb 8 and the other was dated Jan 21 resulting in Discount dates of Feb 18 and Jan 31 respectively (ten days from the invoice date).

# Profit-izing Your Business

For these two invoices, this is what should have happened:

| Invoice # | Invoice Amount | Date Paid should have been | Discount Taken | Paid Amount should have been |
|---|---|---|---|---|
| 1237 | $1,400 | 18-Feb | $28 | $1,372.00 |
| 1346 | $800 | 31-Jan | $16 | $784.00 |
| | | | $44 | |

As a result of paying only these two invoices according to the payment terms offered by the supplier, you would have been $44 richer.

Let's look at another supplier.

Product Company (consider this your main supplier of product that you sell)

During the month you paid this company $10,300 on one invoice. The invoice date was Feb 10 making the discount date Feb 20. You paid the invoice on Feb 17 but did not take the discount. This is what should have happened with this payment.

| Invoice # | Invoice Amount | Date Paid should have been | Discount Taken | Paid Amount should have been |
|---|---|---|---|---|
| 555 | $10,300 | 20-Feb | $206 | $10,094.00 |

Based on this one invoice, if you paid strictly according to the payment terms offered by the supplier, you could have been $206 richer.

Notice that for each of these examples, we said the payment date should have been the last day of the discount period. This is to allow you to hold on to your money as long as possible and possibly earn interest on it in the meantime.

Notice that if all the invoices that were paid during the month had discount terms as stated and you took all the discounts, you would have an additional $543 to spend on other things.

# Profit-izing Your Business

Now, using your own prepared report, how much could you have saved based on the month or sample of payments you choose for analysis? If the answer is zero, then either none of your suppliers offer you discount terms or either you or your accounts payable person is doing a fantastic job and should be congratulated.

What if no one is offering you payment terms? Sometimes in small businesses, the volume you order is not a volume that is considered for discounting. But it never hurts to ask your suppliers about discounts for early payment. You may be surprised and make yourself some money in the process.

Another thing to consider is the volume that will get a discount from the supplier. If you are anywhere near meeting that volume, you may want to consider your ordering practices to get the discount.

**Accounts Payable Aging**

Now, prepare an Accounts Payable Aging Report. This is similar to the Accounts Receivable Aging report you prepared for your receivables. This report should list all the suppliers that you *owe* money to, the amount you owe, a breakdown of amounts and due dates taking into account any terms offered by the supplier. This can be prepared on a spreadsheet by hand or if you use a computer system for your accounts payable, there should be some report that provides this same information, although it may not be called by the same name. Refer to the sample below to help you prepare this report.

# Profit-izing Your Business

| Customer | Amount To Pay | Invoice Number | Invoice Amount | Invoice Date | Date to Pay based on Discount Terms | Terms Date for Full Pay | Discount Percent | Discount Amount if paid on Discount Date | Discount Taken |
|---|---|---|---|---|---|---|---|---|---|
| Sample Company **Accounts Payable Aging Report** | | | | | | | | As of Date 31-Jan-23 | |
| Furniture Company | $2,254 | 235 | $2,300 | 12-Jan | 22-Jan | 11-Feb | 2.00% | $46.00 | |
| ABC Supply Co | $784 | 1346 | $800 | 21-Jan | 31-Jan | 20-Feb | 2.00% | $16.00 | |
| *From here down, these invoices would be added to the report as they are received.* | | | | | | | | | |
| Office Supply Store | $1,045 | 133 | $1,100 | 27-Jan | 6-Feb | 26-Feb | 5.00% | $55.00 | |
| Acme Computers | $582 | 791 | $600 | 1-Feb | 11-Feb | 3-Mar | 3.00% | $18.00 | |
| ABC Supply Co | $1,372 | 1237 | $1,400 | 8-Feb | 18-Feb | 10-Mar | 2.00% | $28.00 | |
| XYZ Supply Co | $5,626 | 743 | $5,800 | 8-Feb | 18-Feb | 10-Mar | 3.00% | $174.00 | |
| Product Company | $10,094 | 555 | $10,300 | 10-Feb | 20-Feb | 12-Mar | 2.00% | $206.00 | |
| Total Payments | $21,757 | | | | | | | | |
| Total Savings from Discounts taken | | | | | | | | $543.00 | |
| Percent of Savings | | | | | | | | 2.50% | |

For this report, I have taken the same invoices that were paid on the Accounts Payable Analysis Report and included them on this aging report.

This report should be prepared as of the end date of each month to give you an idea of what is owed and when it will have to be paid.

Now before anyone mentions that all of these invoices could not have been listed on a report prepared on Jan 31 because some of the invoice dates are in Feb, you are right. The Feb invoices are for illustration purposes. This report can be used as an Accounts Payable control report in the following manner. First you list all the invoices you have as of the day you prepare the report. Assign each invoice a payment date based on the payment terms offered by the supplier. Then add invoices to the report as they arrive in the mail and assign a payment date to each.

Using a Manual System:

**Payment Tickler**

When using a manual system, an easy way to keep track of what has to be paid and when is to use a 31-day tickler file. As the invoice arrives and after recording it on the Accounts Payable Aging / Control Form, simply file the invoice according to the due date calculated based on the payment terms. If you pay your bills every day, just take out what has to be paid three days from now (to allow for delivery time) and pay those bills. If you only want to pay weekly (for instance), on the day you are paying take out all the invoices for the next seven days and pay them.

Computerized Accounts Payable systems make this so much easier by keeping track of the payment due date based on the payment terms and providing you with a report of what invoices need to be paid.

Am I taking advantage of discounts offered?

So, if after your analysis you can answer this "yes", you are taking advantage of discounts offered by the seller. Discounts, as described in the chapter on accounts receivable, work both ways. When you're the one doing the purchasing, you may be able to take a discount based on the seller's terms.

Remember the terms, 2% 10, Net 30 meaning if you pay the invoice within 10 days of the invoice date you can take a 2% discount, otherwise you owe the whole balance within 30 days. Why would you not take the discount?

Taking this discount reduces the amount you pay for the product you sell, thereby increasing your profit.

## What are the general steps to take to control you accounts payable?

Here are some steps you can take to effectively manage your accounts payable:

1. Create a detailed accounts payable policy: Developing an accounts payable policy is the first step to ensuring that your payment process is consistent, efficient, and compliant with your internal controls. Your policy should include details such as payment terms, invoice processing procedures, and late payment penalties.

2. Set up a system for tracking invoices: To avoid losing track of invoices or making late payments, set up a system for tracking your accounts payable. This could be a simple spreadsheet or an accounting software that can automatically categorize and record incoming invoices.

3.  Streamline your payment process: Automating your payment process can help you avoid late payments and save time on manual tasks. Consider implementing an electronic payment system, such as online bill payment, or using accounting software that can automate payment approvals.

4.  Monitor your accounts payable regularly: Monitoring your accounts payable regularly allows you to identify any late payments, payment errors, or discrepancies in your invoice records. Reviewing your accounts payable aging report every week or month can help you stay on top of your payment obligations.

5.  Establish good relationships with vendors: Maintaining good relationships with your vendors can help you avoid payment disputes and ensure that they continue to provide you with the goods and services you need. Be open and transparent about your payment terms and communicate any issues or concerns promptly.

6. Negotiate favorable payment terms: Negotiating payment terms with your vendors can help you manage your cash flow more effectively. Consider negotiating longer payment terms or payment schedules that align with your business's cash flow situation.

7. Implement a budget: Developing and implementing a budget that accounts for your accounts payable expenses can help you avoid overspending and manage your cash flow effectively. Your budget should account for all of your accounts payable obligations, including regular bills and one-time expenses.

By following these steps, you can take control of your accounts payable process and ensure that your business maintains good relationships with vendors while staying financially stable.

# Profit-izing Your Business

# MINIMIZING PURCHASING EXPENSE

### Purchasing defined

Purchasing is the process of acquiring goods or services from an external source to meet the needs of an organization. This involves identifying the goods or services required, selecting suppliers, negotiating contracts, placing orders, receiving goods, and making payment. The purchasing process may involve a variety of stakeholders, including department managers, budget holders, procurement professionals, and suppliers. The overall goal of the purchasing process is to ensure that the organization acquires the goods and services it needs at the best possible price, quality, and delivery time, while managing risks and complying with relevant laws and regulations.

# Profit-izing Your Business

CONCERNING YOUR PURCHASING, ASK YOURSELF THESE QUESTIONS:

✓ Who does the Purchasing?

✓ Do you use Purchase Requisitions? Should you?

✓ Do I have a system in place for analyzing my purchasing and making adjustments?

✓ Do I use automatic purchasing to maintain my inventory or general supplies?

✓ Do I use Procurement Cards? Who uses them?

Let's consider each of these questions in more depth.

## WHO DOES THE PURCHASING FOR THE COMPANY?

Clearly establish who has the authority to initiate a Purchase Order for the company and who makes buying decisions and what information is the decision based on?

Require a purchase order for all purchasing AND/OR provide procurement cards to selected employees for buying specifically defined items locally.

## SHOULD I USED PURCHASE REQUISITIONS?

The difference between a Purchase Requisition and a Purchase Order is significant.

PURCHASE REQUISITIONS should be available to anyone in the company to request that something needs to be purchased. These are usually used for non-inventory items (items that are not for sale to customers) such as office supplies, new equipment, rental equipment, office furnishings, etc.

A Purchase Order is the actual order for the purchase.

Initiating a PURCHASE ORDER should be a very restricted activity within a company because the person who initiates the Purchase Order is spending on behalf of the company.

## DO I HAVE A SYSTEM IN PLACE FOR ANALYZING MY PURCHASING AND MAKING ADJUSTMENTS?

As a business owner, you should insist on seeing and approving every Purchase Order. You should also look at all the purchasing for each month to be sure it was an approved purchase.

## DO I USE AUTOMATIC PURCHASING TO MAINTAIN MY INVENTORY OR GENERAL SUPPLIES?

For maintaining Inventory, an automatic system is a necessity. They can also be used for office supplies if you have a record of what supplies you will need and how often. This is generally not as straight forward as the inventory items.

Negotiate prices on common or popular items for as long a period as is possible.

# Profit-izing Your Business

Minimize number of orders –

Make sure you order in bulk if there is a discount available.

Use dropshipping if that fits in your plan. Dropshipping is a method for satisfying customer orders over the internet. The basic premise is that you put in an order for the product when a customer orders from you. The dropshipping company will ship the product directly to your customer.

## DO I USE PROCUREMENT CARDS?

Provide procurement cards to selected local employees for buying some expendable items locally, such as copy paper, coffee or pods for the office break room, etc.

Procurement cards can be specifically designed to only be used at one store or for one type of purchase.

Any employee who uses a procurement card should be required to get a receipt for the good purchased and turn that into the company for reconciling the procurement card statement each month.

## What controls should be in place for purchasing?

Effective controls are essential in managing purchasing activities. The following are some key controls that should be in place for purchasing:

1. Purchase Requisition: A purchase requisition form should be used to document the need for goods or services before any purchase is made. This form should be approved by an authorized person before the purchase process begins.

2. Purchase Order: A purchase order should be created for every purchase made. It should include details such as the description of the goods or services, quantities, prices, delivery dates, and payment terms.

3. Vendor Selection: A vendor selection process should be in place to ensure that vendors are selected based on objective criteria, such as quality, price, and delivery time. The selection process should also include checks for the vendor's financial stability and reputation.

4. Vendor Approval: Once a vendor has been selected, they should be approved by the purchasing department. This approval should include verifying their business license, tax ID, and insurance coverage.

5. Payment Authorization: An authorized person should approve all payments before they are made. This helps to prevent unauthorized payments and ensures that payments are made in accordance with the agreed-upon terms.

6. Record Keeping: All purchasing activities should be documented and maintained in a central purchasing database. This helps to provide an audit trail and ensures that all purchasing activities are transparent.

7. Contract Management: Contracts should be in place for all purchases, including details such as pricing, payment terms, delivery schedules, and quality standards. Contract management ensures that both parties are aware of their obligations and can help to prevent disputes.

8. By implementing these controls, organizations can ensure that their purchasing activities are efficient, effective, and compliant with relevant laws and regulations.

# Profit-izing Your Business

## What controls should there be over procurement cards?

Procurement cards can be a convenient way to make purchases, but they can also be a source of potential fraud and abuse. Therefore, it is important to have controls in place to ensure that credit cards are used appropriately. Here are some key controls that should be in place for purchasing credit cards:

1. Credit Card Policies: Establish clear policies and procedures for credit card use. These should include guidelines for when credit cards may be used, who is authorized to use them, and what types of purchases are allowed.

2. Credit Card Approval Process: Establish an approval process for issuing credit cards to employees. This should include background checks and credit checks to ensure that employees are trustworthy and financially responsible.

3. Credit Card Limits: Set credit limits for each credit card based on the needs of the employee and the company. This can help prevent overspending and limit the potential damage from fraud or misuse.

4. Receipts and Invoices: Require employees to provide receipts and invoices for all purchases made with credit cards. This ensures that purchases are legitimate and can be tracked and verified.

5. Credit Card Statements: Regularly review credit card statements to identify any unusual activity, errors, or unauthorized purchases. This can help detect potential fraud or misuse.

6. Monthly Reconciliation: Reconcile credit card statements each month to ensure that all purchases made with the credit card are legitimate and authorized.

7. Regular Audits: Conduct regular audits of credit card use and compliance with credit card policies and procedures.

By implementing these controls, organizations can help to prevent credit card fraud and misuse and ensure that credit cards are used appropriately for legitimate business purposes.

## RECEIVING PURCHASED GOODS

This subject refers to who and where the ordered items are received and recorded.

### Using a computerized system:

In the most advanced computerized systems, Use 3- or 4-way matching:

3-way Matching matches the Purchase Order with the Receipt of Goods and the Invoice received from the Supplier. Only quantities that have been received can be paid for through Accounts Payable. This reduces the possibility of you paying in advance for product that you may never receive.

4-way matching adds one more document to the mix, the inspection document. If you order items that need to be inspected before accepting the order, this type of matching should be used. If the inspection determines that the product is not satisfactory or does not work, then this process prevents you from paying for the item(s). Usually in this type of scenario, the item(s) are returned to the supplier for replacement or for credit.

Use Blind Receiving, if possible, i.e. if company is large enough to have a dedicated receiving department. In Blind receiving, the receiver doesn't have any knowledge as to the quantity that has been ordered and should be received. As a result, the receiver has to count every quantity received and enter that quantity in the system.

# Profit-izing Your Business

Because you are using a computerized system, the quantity remaining to be received will be calculated by the system.

Use Standard receiving if necessary or the company does not have a dedicated receiving department. Standard receiving informs the receiver what quantity is still to be received but allows him to receive that quantity or any other.

## Using a manual system

The receiver should count each quantity of each product received and note the received quantity on a copy of the purchase order. The remaining quantity to be received should then be calculated and noted on the PO copy.

If the product requires more detailed inspection before being accepted, the product and the PO copy should be forwarded to the person or department responsible for this inspection.

# Profit-izing Your Business

NOTE: It's important to provide the receiving information to the Accounts Payable department so that they do not pay for items that have not been received.

NOTE 2: If at all possible, never pay for goods not yet received even if you are billed for them. This would be like lending money to your supplier which should be avoided.

# CONTROLLING YOUR INVENTORY

**Inventory defined**

Inventory refers to the collection of goods, materials, or finished products that a business or organization holds in stock to meet customer demand. It can include raw materials, work-in-progress products, finished goods, and spare parts.

Inventory is an essential component of many businesses as it allows them to ensure that they can meet customer demand without experiencing stockouts. Maintaining an optimal level of inventory is important, as too little inventory can result in stockouts and lost sales, while too much inventory can tie up capital and increase storage costs.

## What general controls should there be over the inventory receiving process?

There are several important controls that should be put in place over the inventory receiving process to ensure accuracy, completeness, and security of inventory. Here are some key controls that should be considered:

1. Separation of duties: Different individuals should be responsible for different aspects of the inventory receiving process, such as receiving goods, recording receipts, and updating inventory records. This helps to prevent errors and fraud.

2. Documentation: A formal receiving report should be completed for every shipment received. This report should include details such as the supplier name, date of receipt, quantity received, and condition of goods.

3. Inspection and verification: All goods received should be inspected and verified against the purchase order and packing slip. Any discrepancies should be resolved before inventory records are updated.

4. Security: Adequate security measures should be in place to protect inventory from theft, damage, or unauthorized access. This includes secure storage areas, access controls, and monitoring of inventory movements.

5. Reconciliation: Regular reconciliation of inventory records with physical inventory counts should be performed to identify discrepancies and ensure accurate inventory valuation.

6. Overall, effective controls over the inventory receiving process can help to prevent errors, reduce losses, and ensure the accuracy of inventory records.

# Profit-izing Your Business

Effective inventory management involves balancing the cost of holding inventory with the benefits of having sufficient stock to meet customer demand. This requires careful monitoring of inventory levels, forecasting demand, and establishing inventory policies and procedures to ensure that inventory is ordered, received, and processed efficiently.

This is a major area for cost cutting. Maintaining too much inventory on hand costs dollars for storage costs in addition to the expenditure to get the inventory.

If you are a company that maintains inventory of items that you sell either direct to the public in your own store or on the internet, this chapter will benefit you and possibly help save you some money.

# Profit-izing Your Business

ASK YOURSELF THESE QUESTIONS
CONCERNING YOUR INVENTORY.

- ✓ Am I maintaining too much inventory?
- ✓ Do I have a system in place for analyzing my inventory and making adjustments?
- ✓ Do I use automatic ordering to maintain my inventory?
  - o Minmax planning.
  - o Reorder point planning
- ✓ Do I know how much it costs to maintain my inventory?

Let's consider each of these questions in more depth.

AM I MAINTAINING TOO MUCH
INVENTORY?

So, how do you determine if you are maintaining too much inventory? There are certain methodologies that are used to do this in larger companies; inventory turnover is a high-level indicator of this and inventory aging is another.

Inventory Turnover

What is meant by inventory turnover?

Inventory turnover is a financial ratio that measures how efficiently a company is managing its inventory. It measures the number of times a company sells and replaces its inventory during a specific period, usually a year, but it can be calculated at any time. The formula for inventory turnover is:

Inventory turnover = Cost of goods sold / Average inventory

The cost of goods sold (COGS) is the total cost of the products sold by the company during the period, including the cost of raw materials, direct labor, and manufacturing overhead. Average inventory is calculated by adding the beginning inventory to the ending inventory for the period and dividing the result by 2.

A HIGH INVENTORY TURNOVER RATIO indicates that a company is selling and replacing its inventory quickly, which can be a positive sign of efficient inventory management.

A LOW INVENTORY TURNOVER RATIO, on the other hand, suggests that a company is not selling its inventory quickly enough, which can result in excess inventory, storage costs, and potential write-offs.

It's important to note that <u>inventory turnover ratios can vary widely</u> depending on the industry and the company's business model. Some industries, such as grocery stores, have high inventory turnover ratios due to the perishable nature of their products, while other industries, such as luxury goods, may have lower inventory turnover ratios due to their higher price points and lower demand. This ratio should be compared against industry averages for your type of business. A low turnover implies poor sales and, therefore, excess inventory. A high ratio implies either strong sales or ineffective buying.

High inventory levels are unhealthy because they represent an investment with a rate of return of zero. It also opens the company up to trouble should prices begin to fall.

How is inventory turnover stated in a report?

Inventory turnover is typically stated in a financial report or statement, such as an income statement or balance sheet. It is usually reported as a ratio, expressed as a number of times per year. For example, a company with an inventory turnover ratio of 5 would sell and replace its inventory 5 times per year.

Inventory turnover may also be included in an inventory report, which provides more detailed information about the company's inventory management practices. In an inventory report, inventory turnover may be presented as a ratio, as well as in the form of graphs or charts that illustrate the trend in inventory turnover over time.

# Profit-izing Your Business

Additionally, some companies may benchmark their inventory turnover ratio against industry standards or competitors to evaluate their performance and identify areas for improvement. This may be presented in the form of a comparison chart or table, showing the company's inventory turnover ratio compared to industry benchmarks or competitors.

## DO I HAVE A SYSTEM IN PLACE FOR ANALYZING MY INVENTORY AND MAKING ADJUSTMENTS?

### Average Age of Inventory

The Average Age of Inventory, also known as Days Inventory Outstanding (DIO) or Days to Sell Inventory, is a measure of how long a company holds its inventory before it is sold. It is an important metric in inventory management that can help businesses identify potential issues with their inventory levels and turnover.

# Profit-izing Your Business

The Average Age of Inventory is calculated by dividing the total value of inventory by the cost of goods sold (COGS) per day. The formula is:

Average Age of Inventory = (Total inventory value / COGS) x 365 days

For example, if a company has $1,000,000 worth of inventory and its cost of goods sold per day is $10,000, the average age of inventory would be:

Average Age of Inventory = ($1,000,000 / $10,000) x 365 = 36.5 days

This means that on average, it takes the company 36.5 days to sell its inventory.

# Profit-izing Your Business

The Average Age of Inventory can help businesses identify potential issues with their inventory levels and turnover. A high average age of inventory may indicate that a company is holding onto inventory for too long, which can lead to increased storage costs, obsolescence, and potential write-offs. On the other hand, a low average age of inventory may indicate that a company is not holding enough inventory to meet customer demand.

It's important to note that the Average Age of Inventory can vary widely depending on the industry and the company's business model. Some industries, such as luxury goods, may have a higher average age of inventory due to their higher price points and lower demand, while other industries, such as grocery stores, may have a lower average age of inventory due to the perishable nature of their products.

DO I USE AUTOMATIC ORDERING TO MAINTAIN MY INVENTORY?

There are many types of automatic ordering with inventory. These are the two most used methods – Minmax Planning and Reorder Point Planning.

## Minmax planning defined

Minmax planning is a type of inventory management strategy that helps businesses ensure they have sufficient stock on hand to meet customer demand while minimizing excess inventory and associated costs. This strategy involves establishing minimum and maximum inventory levels for each item in stock and reordering items when the inventory levels reach these thresholds.

The minimum inventory level is the minimum amount of inventory that must be maintained to avoid stockouts, while the maximum inventory level is the maximum amount of inventory that can be held without incurring excessive storage costs. When the inventory level reaches the minimum level, an order is placed to replenish the inventory, and when it reaches the maximum level, no further orders are placed until some of the inventory has been sold or otherwise depleted.

The minmax planning strategy can be used for both raw materials and finished goods inventory. It is often used in industries with seasonal or fluctuating demand, as it allows companies to adjust their inventory levels based on changing demand patterns. It can also help companies optimize their ordering process and reduce the risk of stockouts or overstocking.

One potential drawback of the minmax planning strategy is that it requires accurate forecasting of demand and lead times, as well as careful monitoring of inventory levels to ensure that they stay within the established thresholds. If demand is higher or lower than expected, or lead times are longer than anticipated, the inventory levels may not be sufficient to meet customer demand or may result in excess inventory and associated costs.

## Reorder Point Planning defined

Reorder Point Planning is a popular inventory management strategy that helps businesses determine when to reorder inventory to avoid stockouts. It is a method for calculating the minimum level of inventory that a company needs to have on hand to meet demand until the next order is received.

The reorder point is calculated by taking into account the lead time for ordering inventory, the average rate of sales, and the safety stock level (a buffer of extra inventory to account for unexpected increases in demand or delays in receiving a new shipment). The formula for calculating the reorder point is:

# Profit-izing Your Business

Reorder point = (Average daily usage x Lead time in days) + Safety stock level

For example, if a company sells an average of 20 units per day and the lead time for receiving a new shipment is 10 days, with a safety stock level of 50 units, the reorder point would be:

Reorder point = (20 units/day x 10 days) + 50 units = 250 units

This means that when the inventory level reaches 250 units, it's time to place an order for more inventory to avoid a potential stockout.

Reorder Point Planning can help businesses optimize their inventory levels and avoid stockouts, which can negatively impact customer satisfaction and sales. However, it requires accurate forecasting of demand, lead times, and safety stock levels, as well as close monitoring of inventory levels to ensure that they stay within the established thresholds.

## DO I KNOW HOW MUCH IT COSTS TO MAINTAIN MY INVENTORY?

The costs of maintaining inventory are called the *Carrying Cost of Inventory*
These are the costs of maintaining inventory in a company's warehouse. This includes things like rent, utilities, insurance, taxes, employee costs and the opportunity cost of having your capital tied up in.

There is also a cost for not carrying enough inventory of certain rapidly selling items. These are called Backorder Costs, which is a cost incurred by a business when it is unable to fill an order and must complete it later.

# Profit-izing Your Business

A backorder cost can be discrete, as in the cost to replace a specific piece of inventory, or intangible, such as the effects of poor customer service. Backorder costs are usually computed and displayed on a per-unit basis.

Backorder costs are important for companies to track, as the relationship between holding costs of inventory and backorder costs will determine whether a company should over- or under-produce. If the carrying cost of inventory is less than backorder costs (this is true in most cases), the company should over-produce and keep an inventory.

General Steps for inventory control

Determine your inventory needs: The first step in inventory control is to determine how much inventory you need to have on hand. This will depend on various factors such as the demand for your products, the lead time for restocking, and the amount of space you have available to store inventory. To determine your inventory needs, you

# Profit-izing Your Business

may want to consider using a forecasting method such as
the economic order quantity (EOQ) model. This model
helps you determine the optimal order size for your
inventory based on factors such as demand, lead time, and
carrying costs.

Set reorder points: A reorder point is the point at
which you need to restock your inventory. It is important
to set reorder points for each item in your inventory to
ensure that you always have enough stock to meet
customer demand. To determine your reorder point, you
will need to consider the lead time for restocking, the
demand for the item, and the safety stock you want to have
on hand. Safety stock is a buffer of extra inventory that
you keep on hand to ensure that you don't run out of stock
in the event of unexpected demand or delays in restocking.

Track your inventory: It is important to track your
inventory levels regularly to ensure that you have an

# Profit-izing Your Business

accurate picture of what you have on hand. This can be done manually, by physically counting your inventory and recording the results in a spreadsheet or inventory management software. Alternatively, you can use inventory management software to automate the process of tracking your inventory. This software can track inventory levels in real-time, making it easier to identify when it is time to restock.

   Monitor inventory levels: Regularly monitoring your inventory levels will help you identify when it is time to restock and will also help you spot any potential issues, such as excess inventory or items that are not moving as quickly as expected. You can monitor your inventory levels by comparing your current inventory levels to your reorder points, analyzing sales data to identify trends and changes in demand, and conducting regular physical inventory counts.

# Profit-izing Your Business

Review and adjust your inventory management strategy: As your business grows and changes, it is important to review and adjust your inventory management strategy to ensure that it is still effective. This may involve adjusting your reorder points, implementing new inventory control technologies, or making other changes to your process. You should also review your inventory management strategy regularly to ensure that it is still aligned with your business goals and objectives.

What does an inventory report look like?

An inventory report typically includes information about the items that are held in stock by a company or organization. The specific format and details included in the report can vary depending on the organization's needs and the type of inventory being tracked. However, here are some common elements you might expect to find in an inventory report:

# Profit-izing Your Business

Item description: A brief description of the item being tracked, including the item name, SKU number, or other identifier.

Quantity on hand: The total number of units of each item that are currently in stock.

Quantity sold: The total number of units of each item that have been sold over a specific time period.

Quantity received: The total number of units of each item that have been received from suppliers or other sources over a specific time period.

Cost per unit: The cost per unit of each item, which may include the purchase price, shipping costs, and other expenses.

# Profit-izing Your Business

Total inventory value: The total value of all items currently in stock, which is calculated by multiplying the quantity on hand by the cost per unit.

Stockout status: A flag indicating whether any items are out of stock and unavailable for purchase.

Inventory turnover ratio: The ratio of the cost of goods sold to the average inventory value, which is used to measure how quickly inventory is being sold and replenished.

Aging report: A breakdown of inventory by age, which can help identify items that may be at risk of becoming obsolete or slow-moving.

Reorder points: The minimum quantity of each item that should be maintained in stock to ensure that the organization can meet customer demand without experiencing stockouts.

The above elements are not exhaustive, and the specific details and format of an inventory report can vary based on the requirements of the organization.

Here is a Sample Inventory Report:

| ABC Company | | | | |
| --- | --- | --- | --- | --- |
| Inventory Report as of December 31, 2022 | | | | |
| Item No. | Description | Quantity | Cost/Unit | Total Cost |
| 1 | Widget A | 1,000 | $10.00 | $10,000.00 |
| 2 | Widget B | 500 | $20.00 | $10,000.00 |
| 3 | Widget C | 750 | $15.00 | $11,250.00 |
| 4 | Widget D | 1,250 | $5.00 | $6,250.00 |
| Total: | | 3,500 | | $37,500.00 |
| Inventory Turnover Ratio: 5 | | | | |
| Days Inventory Outstanding (DIO): 73 | | | | |

# Profit-izing Your Business

The following information that is shown cannot be calculated just from this report. Here's how they are calculated:

Inventory Turnover Ratio = Cost of Goods Sold / Average Inventory

DIO = (Average Inventory / Cost of Goods Sold) x 365

Notes:

The inventory turnover ratio of 5 indicates that the company sells and replaces its inventory 5 times per year.

The DIO of 73 indicates that on average, it takes the company 73 days to sell its inventory.

The total cost of inventory is $37,500.00, as of December 31, 2022.

# SIMPLIFYING PAYROLL

## Controls for the payroll process?

There are several controls that should be in place to ensure the accuracy and security of the payroll process. Some of these controls include:

1. Segregation of Duties: The payroll process should be divided into different tasks, and different people should be responsible for each task to reduce the risk of fraud or errors. For example, one person could be responsible for entering employee hours, while another person could be responsible for verifying the accuracy of the data and making the actual payments.

2. Access Control: Access to payroll data and systems should be restricted only to authorized personnel. Access controls should be in place to ensure that only those who need access to payroll information can access it.

3. Audit Trail: There should be a clear and complete audit trail for all payroll transactions. This will help to identify any errors or discrepancies and provide evidence of any fraudulent activity.

4. Regular Reconciliation: Payroll accounts should be regularly reconciled to ensure that the payroll transactions are accurate and complete.

5. Dual Authorization: Any significant changes to payroll data or payments should require dual authorization from two separate individuals to ensure that there is no unauthorized access or tampering.

6. Compliance with Regulations: The payroll process must comply with all relevant laws and regulations, such as tax laws, minimum wage laws, and labor laws.

7. Training and Awareness: All personnel involved in the payroll process should receive training on the proper procedures, controls, and policies. This will help to ensure that they are aware of their responsibilities and can identify any potential issues or risks.

## Other controls to consider:

Avoid payroll advances to your employees. These can indicate an employee who is spending above their income.

Establish formal vacation and holiday rules/pay and keep track of them.

Always pay yourself as part of the payroll, don't rely on just taking money out of the cash register or bank account.

BECAUSE OF THE COMPLEXITY OF PAYROLL AND PAYROLL REPORTING, MANY SMALL BUSINESSES CHOOSE TO USE A PAYROLL PROCESSING SERVICE. THIS IS HIGHLY RECOMMENDED FOR MOST SMALL BUSINESSES.

# Profit-izing Your Business

# NOT SO PETTY CASH

## Controls for Petty Cash?

Petty cash refers to a small amount of cash that is kept on hand by an organization for minor expenses, such as office supplies, postage, or small purchases. To ensure the proper handling and management of petty cash, the following controls should be in place:

1. Establish a Petty Cash Fund:

2. Establish a designated petty cash fund, with a specific amount of money, and assign a custodian to manage the fund.

3. Set Limits:

4. Set limits on the amount of money that can be disbursed from the petty cash fund, and ensure that all disbursements are for legitimate business expenses.

5.  Maintain Detailed Records:

6.  Keep detailed records of all transactions involving the petty cash fund, including the date, amount, purpose, and recipient of each disbursement. This information should be recorded when the cash is handed out. A receipt should be given back by the employee after the purchase along with any change.

7.  Regular Reconciliation:

8.  Reconcile the petty cash fund on a regular basis, typically weekly or monthly, to ensure that the balance in the fund matches the recorded transactions.

9.  Secure Storage:

10. Store the petty cash fund in a secure location, such as a locked safe or drawer, and restrict access to authorized personnel only.

Approval Process:

Establish an approval process for all petty cash disbursements, with authorized personnel required to sign off on each transaction.

Audit Trails:

Maintain clear audit trails of all petty cash transactions, including receipts and other documentation to support the disbursements.

Consider the use of Procurement Cards for some employees who may need to buy locally frequently. The use of a Procurement Card for a purchase should still require a receipt be handed in for reconciling the procurement card account.

By implementing these controls, an organization can help prevent fraud and ensure the proper handling and management of petty cash.

# Profit-izing Your Business

# LOANS TO EMPLOYEES DO'S AND DON'TS

## Controls over loans to employees

If a company offers loans to employees, it is important to establish controls to ensure that the loans are issued fairly and responsibly. Here are some controls that could be put in place:

1.  Written policies:

    The company should have a written policy that outlines the conditions under which employees can apply for loans, the maximum loan amount, the interest rate, the repayment terms, and any other relevant details. This policy should be communicated to all employees.

2.  Loan committee:

The company can establish a loan committee to review loan applications, approve or deny them, and ensure that loans are issued fairly and consistently.

3. Eligibility criteria:

The company can establish clear eligibility criteria for loans, such as minimum length of employment or salary level, to ensure that loans are only issued to employees who are likely to repay them.

4. Approval process:

The company can require loan applications to be approved by multiple levels of management, such as the employee's supervisor and a higher-level manager, to ensure that loans are not issued based on personal relationships.

5. Credit checks:

The company can require credit checks for loan applicants to assess their ability to repay the loan.

6. Repayment monitoring:

> The company should establish a system to monitor loan repayments and ensure that employees are making payments on time. Late payments should be addressed promptly.

7. Audit:

> The company can conduct periodic audits of the loan program to ensure that it is being managed in accordance with established policies and procedures.

By implementing these controls, a company can ensure that its loan program is fair, responsible, and well-managed.

# Profit-izing Your Business

# LOANS TO YOURSELF DO'S AND DON'TS

## Controls over loans to the business owner

There are several controls that can be implemented to manage loans to business owners. Here are a few examples:

1. Establish a loan policy:

A loan policy should be established that outlines the process for loan approval, the types of loans that are available, the interest rates and terms of the loan, and any restrictions or conditions associated with the loan.

2. Require collateral:

Require the business owner to provide collateral as a form of security for the loan. This can be in the form of assets such as property, equipment, or inventory.

3. Credit checks:

# Profit-izing Your Business

Conduct a credit check on the business owner to assess their creditworthiness and ability to repay the loan. This can help identify any potential risks associated with the loan.

4. Loan limit:

Establish a maximum loan limit for business owners. This can help limit the amount of debt the business owner can take on and reduce the risk of default.

5. Regular monitoring:

Regularly monitor the business owner's financial statements and loan repayments to ensure they are meeting their obligations. This can help identify any potential issues early on and enable prompt action to be taken.

6. Independent review:

Consider having an independent party review loan applications and assess the financial health of the business. This can provide an objective view and help identify any potential risks or issues.

# Profit-izing Your Business

Of course, when talking about a small business or a sole proprietor, the owner can take whatever cash they think they need. They shouldn't, however, do this for the sake of the company and the employees who depend on the company for their livelihoods.

# Profit-izing Your Business

# MONTHLY REPORTS RECOMMENDED

There are several financial reports that a small business should have on a monthly basis to track its financial performance and make informed decisions.

The most important are these three.

INCOME STATEMENT

This report shows the business's revenue, expenses, and net income or loss for the month. You must prepare and review an income and expense statement at least monthly. Here's why.

This will show if you made any profit for the month.

## BALANCE SHEET

This report provides an overview of the business's financial position, including its assets, liabilities, and equity. It will show you whether you have more assets than liabilities, i.e. whether you are still solvent or on the verge of bankruptcy.

## CASH FLOW STATEMENT

This report shows the inflows and outflows of cash for the business during the month. It tells you where the cash to pay your bills is coming from, from operations or from reserve cash. If it all came from reserve cash for the month, your business did not make a profit for the month.

## Creating an Income Statement?

An income statement, also known as a profit and loss statement, is a financial document that reports a company's revenues and expenses over a specific period of time, typically a month or a year. The purpose of an income statement is to show a company's profitability and to help stakeholders understand the financial performance of the company.

Here are the steps for creating and reviewing an income statement:

Determine the period of time covered by the income statement: The period of time covered by the income statement is typically a month or a year, but it can be any period of time for which the company wants to report its financial performance. This period is called the reporting period.

Gather the necessary financial data: To create an income statement, you will need to gather all of the financial data that relates to the reporting period. This includes revenues, expenses, and any other financial

# Profit-izing Your Business

transactions that have occurred during the period. The financial data should be organized in a clear and logical manner, such as by type of revenue or expense.

Organize the financial data: An income statement typically starts with revenues at the top and lists the various types of revenues that the company has earned during the reporting period. Below the revenues, the income statement lists the various types of expenses that the company has incurred during the period. The net income (profit or loss) is calculated by subtracting the total expenses from the total revenues.

Calculate the net income: To calculate the net income, you will need to add up all of the revenues and subtract all of the expenses. The result will be either a profit or a loss, depending on whether the revenues exceeded the expenses.

# Profit-izing Your Business

Review the income statement: After the income statement has been prepared, it is important to review it carefully to understand the company's financial performance and to identify any trends or issues that need to be addressed. This might include analyzing the revenues and expenses to see which areas are contributing most to the company's profitability, and looking for any unusual or unexpected items that might require further investigation.

Use the income statement to make informed decisions: The income statement can be a valuable tool for making informed decisions about the company's future financial performance. For example, if the company is experiencing declining revenues or increasing expenses, it may be necessary to implement changes to improve profitability. On the other hand, if the company is experiencing strong financial performance, it may be possible to invest in growth or expansion opportunities.

# Profit-izing Your Business

Here is an example of what an income statement might look like:

| ABC COMPANY | | |
|---|---|---|
| 1 **Income and Expense Statement** (also called Profit and Loss Statement) | | |
| 2 For the Year Ended December 31, 2022 | | |
| 3 | | |
| 4 Revenue: | | |
| 5   Sales | $500,000 | |
| 6   Other revenue | $50,000 | |
| 7 Total revenue | | $550,000 |
| 8 | | |
| 9 Cost of Goods Sold: | | |
| 10   Beginning inventory | $100,000 | |
| 11   Purchases | $200,000 | |
| 12   Ending inventory | ($50,000) | |
| 13 Total cost of goods sold | | $250,000 |
| 14 | | |
| 15 Gross Profit  (Line 7 minus Line 13) | | $300,000 |
| 16 | | |
| 17 Operating Expenses: | | |
| 18   Rent | $50,000 | |
| 19   Salaries and wages | $100,000 | |
| 20   Advertising | $25,000 | |
| 21   Supplies | $15,000 | |
| 22   Depreciation | $10,000 | |
| 23   Other expenses | $5,000 | |
| 24 Total operating expenses | | $205,000 |
| 25 Operating Income  (Line 15 minus Line 24) | | $95,000 |
| 26 | | |
| 27 Interest Expense | | ($5,000) |
| 28 | | |
| 29 Net Income  (Line 25 minus Line 27) | | $90,000 |

In this example, the company had total revenue of $550,000 for the year ended December 31, 2022. The cost of goods sold was $250,000, leaving a gross profit of $300,000. After subtracting operating expenses of

$205,000 and interest expense of $5,000, the company had net income of $90,000 for the year.

## Creating a Balance Sheet?

A balance sheet is a financial statement that provides a snapshot of a company's financial position at a specific point in time. It shows what a company owns (assets), what it owes (liabilities), and what remains for the owners of the company (equity).

A typical balance sheet is divided into two main sections: assets and liabilities & equity. Here's an example of what a basic balance sheet might look like:

| XYZ Company | | |
| --- | --- | --- |
| Balance Sheet as of December 31, 2022 | | |
| **Assets:** | | |
| Cash and cash equivalents | 10000 | |
| Accounts receivable | 15000 | |
| Inventory | 20000 | |
| Property, plant, and equipment | 50000 | |
| Intangible assets | 5000 | |
| Other assets | 2000 | |
| **Total assets** | | 102000 |
| **Liabilities:** | | |
| Accounts payable | 5000 | |
| Accrued expenses | 2000 | |
| Short-term debt | 8000 | |
| Long-term debt | 30000 | |
| **Total Liabilities:** | | 45000 |
| **Equity:** | | |
| Common stock | 50000 | |
| Retained earnings | 7000 | |
| **Owner's or Shareholders' equity:** | | 57000 |
| **Total liabilities and equity** | | 102000 |

In this example, the company has $102,000 in total assets, which is equal to the total liabilities and equity. The company has a mix of current assets like cash and accounts receivable, as well as long-term assets like property and equipment. On the liabilities and equity side, the company has a mix of current liabilities like accounts payable and short-term debt, as well as long-term liabilities like long-term debt. The shareholders' equity section shows the amount of funding the company has received from investors, as well as any earnings that have been retained in the business.

The balance sheet equation is Assets = Liabilities + Equity, which means that the total value of the assets must equal the total value of the liabilities and equity. This balance is represented on the balance sheet by showing the total assets on one side and the total liabilities and equity on the other side.

## Creating a Cash Flow Statement?

A cash flow statement is a financial statement that provides information about the cash inflows and outflows of a company during a specific period of time. It is divided into three main sections: operating activities, investing activities, and financing activities. Each section provides information about the cash flows related to a specific type of activity.

The example below shows how a company's net income of $50,000 is adjusted by non-cash items such as depreciation and changes in working capital, resulting in a net cash flow from operating activities of $50,000. The investing activities section shows that the company spent $20,000 on property, plant, and equipment, but received $15,000 from the sale of long-term investments, resulting in a net cash outflow of $5,000. The financing activities section shows that the company raised $30,000 through the issuance of common stock but paid $5,000 to repay long-term debt and $10,000 in dividends, resulting in a net cash inflow of $15,000. Finally, the net increase in cash and cash equivalents for the year is $60,000, which is added to the cash and cash equivalents at the beginning of the year

# Profit-izing Your Business

to arrive at the cash and cash equivalents at the end of the year.

Here's an example of a cash flow statement for a hypothetical company:

| | ABC COMPANY | | |
|---|---|---|---|
| | CASH FLOW STATEMENT | | |
| | Year (or Month) Ended December 31, 2022 | | |
| 1 | Cash flows from operating activities: | | |
| 2 | Net income | $50,000 | |
| 3 | Depreciation and amortization | $10,000 | |
| 4 | Increase in accounts receivable | ($20,000) | |
| 5 | Increase in inventory | ($30,000) | |
| 6 | Increase in accounts payable | $15,000 | |
| 7 | Net cash provided by operating activities | | $25,000 |
| 8 | | | |
| 9 | Cash flows from investing activities: | | |
| 10 | Purchase of property, plant, and equipment | ($20,000) | |
| 11 | Proceeds from sale of long-term investments | $5,000 | |
| 12 | Net cash used in investing activities | | ($15,000) |
| 13 | | | |
| 14 | Cash flows from financing activities: | | |
| 15 | Proceeds from issuance of common stock | $10,000 | |
| 16 | Payment of long-term debt | ($25,000) | |
| 17 | Payment of dividends | ($5,000) | |
| 18 | Net cash used in financing activities | | ($20,000) |
| 19 | | | |
| 20 | Net increase in cash and cash equivalents | | $5,000 |
| 21 | (Line 7 Plus Line 12 plus Line 18) | | |
| 22 | | | |
| 23 | Cash and cash equivalents at beginning of year | | $30,000 |
| 24 | | | |
| 25 | Cash and cash equivalents at end of year | | $35,000 |

Here is more detail on each item.

# Profit-izing Your Business

This cash flow statement shows the company's cash inflows and outflows for the year ended December 31, 2022. The operating activities section shows that the company had net income of $50,000, but had increases in accounts receivable, inventory, and accounts payable, which resulted in a net cash inflow from operating activities of $25,000.

The investing activities section shows that the company spent $20,000 on property, plant, and equipment, but received $5,000 from the sale of long-term investments, resulting in a net cash outflow of $15,000.

The financing activities section shows that the company raised $10,000 through the issuance of common stock but paid $25,000 to reduce long-term debt and $5,000 in dividends, resulting in a net cash outflow of $20,000.

# Profit-izing Your Business

Finally, the net increase in cash and cash equivalents for the year is $5,000, which is added to the cash and cash equivalents at the beginning of the year to arrive at the cash and cash equivalents at the end of the year, which is $35,000.

## OTHER MONTHLY FINANCIAL REPORTS

In addition to the three reports mentioned, there are some others that also need to be produced for review each month.

These reports include:

Accounts Receivable Aging Report: This report shows the status of customer invoices and how long they have been outstanding. This is discussed in much more detail in the chapter on Accounts Receivable.

# Profit-izing Your Business

Accounts Payable Aging Report: This report shows the status of vendor invoices and how long they have been outstanding. This is discussed in much more detail in the chapter on Accounts Payable.

Inventory Report: This report shows the value of the company's inventory at the end of the month. This is discussed in much more detail in the chapter on Inventory.

Sales Report: This report shows the business's sales for the month by product, service, or customer. This is discussed in much more detail in the chapter on Customer Orders.

Expenses Report: This report shows the business's expenses for the month, broken down by category. Whereas the Income Statement shows expenses by category, this report shows the detail of all expenses.

Budget to Actual Report: This report compares totals of expenses by category to your budgeted figures for the same category. Any significant differences should be explained.

By reviewing these reports on a monthly basis, small business owners can gain a better understanding of their financial performance and make informed decisions to improve their operations.

## What does an accounts receivable aging report look like?

See the chapter on Accounts Receivable for a detail explanation of this report.

## What does an accounts payable aging report look like?

See the chapter on Accounts Receivable for a detail explanation of this report.

## What does a monthly sales report look like?

A monthly sales report can vary depending on the organization and the industry. However, some common elements that are typically included in a monthly sales report are:

1. Overview of the period: A brief summary of the sales performance for the month, including key metrics such as total sales revenue, number of units sold, and average order value.

2. Comparison with the previous month: A comparison of the current month's sales performance with the previous

# Profit-izing Your Business

month's sales performance, highlighting any changes and trends.

3. Comparison with the same period last year: A comparison of the current month's sales performance with the same period last year, highlighting any changes and trends.

4. Sales by product or service: A breakdown of sales by product or service, including the total sales revenue and the number of units sold for each product or service.

5. Sales by region: A breakdown of sales by region, including the total sales revenue and the number of units sold for each region.

6. Sales by customer: A breakdown of sales by customer, including the total sales revenue and the number of units sold for each customer.

7. Sales goals and performance: An overview of the sales goals set for the month and how well the team performed against these goals.

8. Opportunities and challenges: A discussion of any opportunities or challenges that impacted sales performance during the month.

Next steps: A summary of any action items or next steps based on the sales performance for the month.

Overall, a monthly sales report should provide a clear and concise overview of the sales performance for the month and help identify areas for improvement or opportunities for growth.

## What does a monthly expenses report look like?

A monthly expenses report typically includes a list of all the expenses incurred during the month, categorized by type of expense (such as rent/mortgage, utilities, food, entertainment, transportation, etc.). The report may also include the total amount spent in each category and the percentage of the total budget spent in each category.

Some common elements you might see in a monthly expenses report include:

1. Total income: This is the total amount of money earned during the month.

2. Total expenses: This is the total amount of money spent during the month.

3. Itemized expenses: This includes a detailed list of all the expenses incurred during the month, along with the date of the transaction and the amount spent. Expenses may be categorized in different ways, depending on the needs of the person or organization creating the report.

4. Summary of expenses: This section provides a summary of the expenses by category, along with the percentage of the total budget spent in each category.

5. Budget vs. Actual: This section compares the budgeted amount for each category to the actual amount spent, to see if there were any variances.

Notes: This section may include any additional information or comments that could help explain certain expenses or variances in the budget.

A relatively easy method for producing your monthly expenses report is to use the same format as for your monthly Income and Expense Statement. Rather than just reporting one month, use a spreadsheet so you can add additional months to the report and a column each moth for the actual budgeted amount for each category. A third column for each month should show the variance in the actual to budget. This report would look like this:

# Profit-izing Your Business

| | ABC COMPANY | January Actual | Budget | Variance | % |
|---|---|---|---|---|---|
| | Income and Expense Statement with Budget to Actual | | | | |
| 1 | Income and Expense Statement with Budget to Actual | | | | |
| 2 | For the Month Ends in 2023 | | | | |
| 3 | | January Actual | Budget | Variance | % |
| 4 | Revenue: | | | | |
| 5 | Sales | $50,000 | $47,200 | $2,800 | 5.6 |
| 6 | Other revenue | $5,000 | $3,750 | $1,250 | 25.0 |
| 7 | Total revenue | $55,000 | $50,950 | $4,050 | 7.4 |
| 8 | | | | | |
| 9 | Cost of Goods Sold: | | | | |
| 10 | Beginning inventory | $10,000 | $10,000 | $0 | 0.0 |
| 11 | Purchases | $20,000 | $15,800 | $4,200 | 21.0 |
| 12 | Ending inventory | $5,000 | $7,500 | ($2,500) | (50.0) |
| 13 | Total cost of goods sold | $25,000 | $18,300 | $6,700 | 26.8 |
| 14 | | | | | |
| 15 | Gross Profit (Line 7 minus Line 13) | $30,000 | $32,650 | ($2,650) | (8.8) |
| 16 | | | | | |
| 17 | Operating Expenses: | | | | |
| 18 | Rent | $5,000 | $5,000 | $0 | 0.0 |
| 19 | Salaries and wages | $10,000 | $9,760 | $240 | 2.4 |
| 20 | Advertising | $2,500 | $2,780 | ($280) | (11.2) |
| 21 | Supplies | $1,500 | $1,260 | $240 | 16.0 |
| 22 | Depreciation | $1,000 | $1,000 | $0 | 0.0 |
| 23 | Other expenses | $500 | $230 | $270 | 54.0 |
| 24 | Total operating expenses | $20,500 | $20,030 | $470 | 2.3 |
| 25 | Operating Income (Line 15 minus Line 24) | $9,500 | $12,620 | ($3,120) | (32.8) |
| 26 | | | | | |
| 27 | Interest Expense | $500 | $540 | ($40) | (8.0) |
| 28 | | | | | |
| 29 | Net Income (Line 25 minus Line 27) | $9,000 | $12,080 | ($3,080) | (34.2) |

Let's look at some items on this report.

Notice that your Total Revenue for January is up 7.4% over your budgeted amount for the month. More revenue than you expected is always good.

But look a little further at the Gross Profit. It's down compared to the budget 8.8%. How can this be explained?

# Profit-izing Your Business

Review the Cost of Goods Sold (COGS) section. Note that your Purchases are up 21% for the month compared to budget. This is reflected negatively in the Gross Profit because it has increased your COGS.

Reviewing the Operating Expenses, note that your Advertising Expense is down 11.2% but you Supplies and Other Expenses are up 16% and 54% respectively. This has added to your Total Operating Expenses and further impacted your Operating Income and, of course, your Net Income.

NOTE: Reviewing these items for a one-month period doesn't necessarily mean that anything is wrong with your company operations. Variances between Budgeted and Actual Amounts is to be expected. What this review shows is items that you may want to keep an eye on. The next monthly review could show that these issues were isolated, or it could identify further issues to watch.

# Profit-izing Your Business

The purpose of this review is simply to show how to review Budget to Actual.

Overall, a monthly income and expenses report and a comparison to actual expenses is a useful tool for tracking spending and identifying areas where adjustments can be made to improve financial management.

# Profit-izing Your Business

# FIND THE PERFECT LOCATION

## What are the things to remember when selecting a location for your business?

The location of your business can have a considerable impact on the profitability.

When selecting a location for your business, there are several key factors to consider:

1. Proximity to customers: Consider whether the location is easily accessible to your target customer base. Do you rely on walk in traffic? If so, does your location lend itself to this? Can you get foot traffic from other businesses in the area? Do you need parking for customers or fleet vehicles?

2. Competition: Consider the level of competition in the area and whether there is room for your business to succeed.

3. Zoning regulations: Make sure the location is zoned for the type of business you plan to operate.

4. Cost: Consider the cost of renting or purchasing the space, as well as any additional costs such as utilities and property taxes.

5. Access to transportation: Consider whether the location is easily accessible by car, public transportation, or other modes of transportation.

6. Access to employees: Consider whether the location is easily accessible for potential employees and whether there is a sufficient pool of qualified candidates in the area.

7. Amenities: Consider whether the location has access to amenities such as restaurants, hotels, and other services that may be useful to your business or employees.

8. Potential for growth: Consider whether the location has the potential to support the growth of your business over time.

# Profit-izing Your Business

# ADVERTISING AND MARKETING – KNOW THE DIFFERENCE

## What is advertising versus marketing?

Advertising and marketing are related concepts, but they are not the same thing. Advertising is a specific component of marketing that involves promoting a product or service.

Marketing involves researching and identifying customer needs, developing products or services that meet those needs, pricing the products or services, promoting the products or services, and distributing them to customers.

# Profit-izing Your Business

Advertising is a part of marketing that involves promoting products or services through various channels, while marketing encompasses a broader set of activities that includes product development, pricing, promotion, and distribution.

Simply stated, advertising is promoting a product or service whereas, marketing is promoting your company itself. A good example of marketing is joining your local Chamber of Commerce and local business associations and participating in their meetings and events. This helps get your company name out in the community.

## Methods of Advertising

There are many different methods of advertising, and the most effective method for a particular business will depend on various factors such as the target audience, budget, and marketing objectives. Here are some common methods of advertising:

# Profit-izing Your Business

1. Television advertising:

   This is a popular method of advertising, as it allows businesses to reach a large audience with a single ad. However, it can be expensive to produce and air TV ads.

2. Print advertising:

   This includes advertisements in newspapers, magazines, brochures, and flyers. Print ads can be cost-effective, especially for small businesses targeting local markets.

3. Outdoor advertising:

   This includes billboards, posters, and signs. Outdoor advertising can be effective for businesses targeting a specific geographical area.

4. Radio advertising:

   Radio ads can be a cost-effective way to reach a targeted audience, especially for businesses with a limited budget.

5. Online advertising:

> This includes various forms of digital advertising such as banner ads, social media ads, pay-per-click (PPC) ads, and search engine marketing (SEM). Online advertising can be highly targeted and cost-effective.

6. Influencer marketing:

> This involves partnering with social media influencers to promote a product or service. Influencer marketing can be effective for businesses targeting a specific niche audience.

7. Content marketing:

> This involves creating valuable content such as blog posts, videos, and social media posts to attract and engage an audience. Content marketing can be a cost-effective way to build brand awareness and generate leads.

8. Event marketing:

This involves sponsoring or hosting events to promote a product or service. Event marketing can be effective for businesses looking to generate leads or build brand awareness.

9. Direct mail advertising:

This includes sending promotional materials such as flyers or catalogs directly to potential customers via mail. Direct mail advertising can be effective for businesses targeting a specific geographic area or demographic.

## Marketing activities

Marketing activities can vary depending on the nature of the business and the target market. Here are some specific marketing activities that businesses might engage in:

1. Market research: This involves gathering data and analyzing the market to understand customer needs, preferences, and behaviors.

2. Product development: This involves creating new products or improving existing ones to better meet customer needs and preferences.

3. Pricing: This involves setting prices for products or services based on market demand, competition, and production costs.

4. Promotion: This involves promoting products or services through advertising, sales promotions, public relations, and other communication channels.

5. Distribution: This involves getting products or services to customers through various channels such as retail stores, e-commerce websites, and distribution centers.

6. Branding: This involves creating a unique brand identity that distinguishes the business from its competitors and appeals to its target market.

7. Content marketing: This involves creating and sharing valuable content such as blog posts, videos, and social media posts to attract and engage an audience.

8. Influencer marketing: This involves partnering with social media influencers to promote a product or service.

9. Customer relationship management (CRM): This involves managing customer interactions and relationships to improve customer satisfaction and loyalty.

10. Sales management: This involves managing the sales process, including lead generation, prospecting, qualifying leads, and closing sales.

# Profit-izing Your Business

# SMALL BUSINESS COMPUTER SYSTEMS

There are three areas where a typical small business including a sole proprietor can use computer software to help in the business.

These three areas are:

1 . Accounting software

2 . Point of sale system

3. Back-office software for letters, advertising,

## ACCOUNTING SOFTWARE

## What accounting software is recommended for small business?

There are several accounting software options available for small businesses. Some of the most popular ones include:

QuickBooks (https://quickbooks.intuit.com/): This is one of the most widely used accounting software options for small businesses. It offers a range of features including invoicing, expense tracking, payroll processing, and tax preparation. This may be too much for the typical small business. Monthly Subscription required for cloud based. Cloud based and Downloadable versions available.

Simple planning (https://www.simpleplanning.com) : This is a simple accounting system that includes recording income and expenses as well as invoicing. It is based on Microsoft Excel and is excellent for a new, small business. No monthly subscription. If you buy the premium version, updates are included. Free Downloadable Demo version. Downloadable, no cloud-based version.

Xero (https://www.xero.com/): This is a cloud-based accounting software that is popular among small businesses. It offers features such as invoicing, bank reconciliation, and expense tracking. Cloud based, no downloadable version. Monthly subscription required.

FreshBooks (https://www.freshbooks.com/): This is another cloud-based accounting software that is easy to use and offers features such as invoicing, time tracking, and project management. Cloud based, no downloadable version. Monthly subscription required.

# Profit-izing Your Business

Zoho Books (https://www.zoho.com/us/books): This is a cloud-based accounting software that offers features such as invoicing, expense tracking, and project management. Cloud based, no downloadable version. Monthly subscription required. There is a free starter version.

Wave (https://www.waveapps.com/): This is a free accounting software that offers features such as invoicing, accounting, and receipt scanning.

When choosing an accounting software for your small business, consider your specific needs, budget, and ease of use. I encourage you to use the links provided to look at each of these offerings in more detail. It's also a good idea to read reviews and compare features before making a final decision.

If you use a bookkeeping or accounting firm to do your books, you may want to have the same software they have. It makes it easier to transfer files between the two of you.

One other point. Cloud based means you have no software on your computer. This also means you have none of your accounting data on your computer. For this to be useful, you must have an excellent internet connection. If you're nervous about putting all your accounting data in the cloud, look for a downloadable version of accounting software.

## POINT-OF-SALE SYSTEM

### So, what is a point of sale system?

A point of sale (POS) system is a computerized system used by businesses to process sales transactions. It typically includes hardware such as a cash register, barcode scanner, and payment terminal, as well as software to manage inventory, track sales data, and process payments.

A POS system can also include additional features like customer relationship management (CRM), employee management, and analytics to help businesses make informed decisions about their operations. POS systems are used in a wide range of industries, including retail, hospitality, and healthcare. Some small businesses should use them to make their sales and income processing easier to track.

## What are some retail point of sale systems for small businesses?

There are many retail point of sale (POS) systems available for small businesses. Here are a few popular options:

# Profit-izing Your Business

Eposnow (https://www.waveapps.com/): Epos Now is a cloud-based point of sale (POS) system designed for small to medium-sized businesses. Overall, Epos Now is a feature-rich POS system that can help businesses manage their sales, inventory, and customer data more efficiently. It's a good option for businesses that need a comprehensive POS system with a range of features and integrations.

Square POS (https://squareup.com/): Square is a popular and affordable POS system that can be used on a smartphone or tablet. It offers a range of features including inventory management, sales reporting, and customer management.

Lightspeed Retail (https://www.lightspeedhq.com/) : Lightspeed is a cloud-based POS system that can be used on a tablet or desktop computer. It offers features like inventory management, customer management, and analytics.

Clover POS (https://www.clover.com/pricing/station-duo): Clover is a popular POS system that can be used on an Android or iOS device. It offers features like inventory management, employee management, and customer management.

When choosing a POS system for your small business, consider your specific needs and budget, and look for a system that offers the features and integrations that are most important to you.

## Difference between a cash register and a Point of sale system

A cash register and a point of sale (POS) system are both used for processing transactions and managing sales, but there are some key differences between them:

Functionality:

A cash register is primarily used to calculate and record sales transactions. It can handle cash payments and provide a basic record of sales. On the other hand, a POS system can handle a wider range of payment methods (such as credit/debit cards, mobile payments, and gift cards), manage inventory and customer data, generate reports, and provide analytics on sales performance. If you also do some cash sales, you will also need a cash drawer but this can be separate from your POS.

Connectivity:

Cash registers are typically standalone machines that don't connect to other systems or devices. POS systems, on the other hand, are often cloud-based and can be integrated with other systems and devices, such as barcode scanners, receipt printers, and accounting software.

Cost:

Cash registers are usually less expensive than POS systems, but they also offer fewer features and functionalities. POS systems can be more expensive, but they can provide a greater return on investment over time, particularly for businesses that need to manage inventory, analyze sales data, and offer a variety of payment options.

Overall, while cash registers are suitable for very small businesses with low transaction volumes, most businesses prefer a POS system for its greater functionality, connectivity, and scalability.

## BACK OFFICE SOFTWARE

Some definitions of back-office software include everything that is not used for selling your product or service which would include the accounting system and the point-of-sale system.

For our purposes, this category is the software used for support purposes within the company.

This includes, word processing, spreadsheets, brochures, advertising material, presentations, email, etc.

Applications such as Microsoft Office, Google Apps, LibreOffice, etc.

Google Apps and Libre Office have completely free versions while Microsoft Office 365 is an annual subscription service at a reasonable price.

# Profit-izing Your Business

# CONTROL PROCEDURES THAT MAKE SENSE

Any company must have certain controls in place to avoid being ripped off by employees and customers. This is not to say that all employees and customers are out to steal from you; most, I believe, are honest and would never do that. You must protect yourself from the few bad actors just in case.

I've mentioned many control points throughout this book that should be implemented by any size business. There are several key control procedures and processes that a company should have in place to ensure the efficient and effective management of its operations. In this chapter I have summarized the significant control processes and procedures in each area.

## Major Control Procedures

Internal controls:

Internal controls are the policies and procedures that a company has in place to ensure the accuracy and reliability of financial reporting, compliance with laws and regulations, and the safeguarding of assets. These controls include things like segregation of duties, regular monitoring of financial transactions, and the use of physical and electronic security measures.

Risk management:

Risk management involves identifying, assessing, and mitigating the risks that a company faces in its operations. This process includes identifying potential risks, assessing the likelihood and impact of those risks, and implementing strategies to mitigate or manage those risks.

Budgeting and forecasting:

A company should have a well-defined process for creating and managing its budget, as well as for forecasting its financial performance. This process should include regular monitoring of actual performance against budget and forecasting assumptions and making adjustments as needed. The adjustments that are made should not adjust the budget but should concentrate on why an actual amount (income or expense) differs significantly from the budgeted amount. All of these major differences should be documented and explained.

Performance measurement and evaluation:

A company should have a system for measuring and evaluating the performance of its employees, departments, and business units. This includes setting clear goals and objectives, providing regular feedback and coaching, and conducting performance evaluations on a regular basis.

Information technology controls:

Information technology controls are the policies and procedures that a company has in place to ensure the security, confidentiality, and integrity of its electronic data. This includes things like access controls, backup and recovery procedures, and regular monitoring of system activity.

Compliance monitoring:

A company should have a system for monitoring compliance with laws, regulations, and company policies. This includes regular internal audits, training programs, and reporting systems to ensure that all employees are aware of their responsibilities and are adhering to company policies.

Asset management:

A company should have a system for managing its assets, including equipment, inventory, and property. This includes regular tracking and monitoring of asset location and status, as well as implementing procedures for the disposal of assets when they are no longer needed.

# Profit-izing Your Business

These are just some of the major control procedures and processes that a company should have in place. The specific controls that a company needs will depend on its size, industry, and other factors.

# Profit-izing Your Business

# DON'T FORGET YOUR EMPLOYEES

Always remember your employees are the heart of your business. Employee benefits are a crucial aspect of any company's strategy to retain its employees.

Here are some benefits, other than a decent income, that you can offer to keep your employees from leaving:

Health and wellness benefits:

Employees value benefits that promote their well-being, such as health insurance, gym memberships, mental health counseling, and wellness programs. By offering these benefits, you can show your employees that you care about their health and happiness, which can boost morale and loyalty.

# Profit-izing Your Business

Flexible work arrangements:

Offering flexible work arrangements, such as telecommuting, flexible hours, or job-sharing, can help employees balance their work and personal lives. This can be especially important for working parents or employees with caregiving responsibilities.

Professional development opportunities:

Employees want to know that their employer is invested in their growth and development. Offering opportunities for training, career development, and mentorship can help your employees build their skills and advance their careers within your organization. Helping to pay for an employee's school expenses while they're studying for a college degree, or a certificate is a good example.

Retirement benefits:

Retirement benefits, such as 401(k) plans or pensions, can provide your employees with long-term financial security. By offering these benefits, you can help your employees plan for their future and demonstrate that you are committed to their well-being beyond their time at your organization.

Employee recognition programs:

Employees want to feel valued and appreciated for their contributions to the organization. Offering employee recognition programs, such as bonuses, awards, or public recognition, can help boost morale and reinforce the value of your employees' work.

Remember, every organization is unique, and the benefits that are most effective at retaining your employees will depend on your company culture, industry, and the needs of your employees.

# Profit-izing Your Business

# YOUR MUST-DO DAILY ACTION PLAN

The Daily Action Plan for Keeping Your Business Running Smoothly and Profitably.

Review your Receivables every morning to see what companies are behind in their payments, what payments were received and posted and what is still outstanding.

Review your Do Not Sell to List to determine if any company can be removed from it and if any other companies need to be added based on outstanding past due invoices.

Review your Watch List to see if any changes need to be made to it based on yesterday's activity.

# Profit-izing Your Business

Review your Payables to make sure you are paying promptly and taking the discount offered by your vendors.

# YOUR MUST-DO MONTHLY ACTION PLAN

On a monthly basis , a business owner should take the time to perform several tasks.

Doing these will ensure that the business is running smoothly from a financial point of view and will help identify any issues that need to be addressed before they get out of hand.

## REVIEW YOUR INCOME STATEMENT

Reviewing your income statement is an essential task for any business owner or individual who wants to keep track of their financial performance.

Here are some steps you can follow to review your income statement:

# Profit-izing Your Business

Review the revenue section:

This section shows how much money your business has earned during a specific period. Make sure all the revenue sources are listed accurately and that there are no duplicate entries.

Check the cost of goods sold (COGS):

This section shows the direct costs of producing the goods or services that you sell. Ensure that the COGS is calculated correctly and that it is in line with industry standards.

Analyze gross profit:

The gross profit is the revenue minus the COGS. This figure shows how much money your business is making after accounting for the direct costs of production. Check whether the gross profit is sufficient to cover your operating expenses.

# Profit-izing Your Business

Review operating expenses:

This section shows the indirect costs of running your business, such as rent, utilities, salaries, marketing expenses, and other overhead costs. Ensure that all expenses are accurately recorded and that there are no unauthorized or unnecessary expenses.

Check net income:

The net income is the final figure that shows how much money your business has earned or lost during the period. If your net income is positive, it means that your business is profitable, while a negative net income means that your business is operating at a loss, at least for the month.

Compare to previous periods:

# Profit-izing Your Business

To get a better understanding of your business's financial performance, compare your income statement to previous periods. Look for trends and patterns in revenue, expenses, and net income.

Seek professional advice:

If you're not sure how to review your income statement or need help interpreting the figures, consider seeking the advice of a professional accountant or financial advisor. They will be able to explain any questions you may have.

By following these steps, you can ensure that your income statement is accurate, complete, and provides valuable insights into your business's financial performance.

REVIEW BALANCE SHEET

There are several ratios that can be calculated using the information on a balance sheet that can help provide insights into a company's financial health and performance. Here are some important ratios to keep an eye on.

Current Ratio:

This is a liquidity ratio that measures a company's ability to meet its short-term obligations with its current assets. It is calculated by dividing current assets by current liabilities. A ratio of 1 or greater is considered favorable.

Debt-to-Equity Ratio:

This is a leverage ratio that measures a company's level of debt relative to its equity. It is calculated by

# Profit-izing Your Business

dividing total liabilities by total equity. A lower ratio indicates less financial risk.

Gross Profit Margin:

This is a profitability ratio that measures the percentage of sales revenue that exceeds the cost of goods sold. It is calculated by dividing gross profit by sales revenue. A higher margin indicates better profitability.

Return on Equity (ROE):

This is a profitability ratio that measures the return generated on owners' or shareholders' equity. It is calculated by dividing net income by total equity. A higher ROE indicates better profitability.

Asset Turnover Ratio:

This is an efficiency ratio that measures a company's ability to generate sales from its assets. It is calculated by

# Profit-izing Your Business

dividing sales revenue by total assets. A higher ratio indicates better efficiency.

Quick Ratio:

This is a liquidity ratio that measures a company's ability to meet its short-term obligations with its most liquid assets. It is calculated by dividing current assets minus inventory by current liabilities. A ratio of 1 or greater is considered favorable.

These ratios can provide a quick snapshot of a company's financial health and performance, but it's important to consider them in context and also to look at other financial statements, such as the income statement and cash flow statement, to get a complete picture.

REVIEW CASHFLOW STATEMENT

# Profit-izing Your Business

The cash flow statement is a financial report that provides information on the cash inflows and outflows of a company during a particular period. It is an important tool for investors, creditors, and management in understanding the financial health of a business.

The statement is divided into three sections: operating activities, investing activities, and financing activities.

Operating activities:

These refer to the cash inflows and outflows related to the primary business operations of the company, such as sales and expenses. It is important to closely examine this section as it provides insights into the cash generated from the core business activities of the company.

Investing activities:

These refer to the cash inflows and outflows related to the purchase or sale of assets, such as property, plant, and equipment or investments in other companies. This section is important as it provides information on the company's investments and capital expenditures.

Financing activities:

These refer to the cash inflows and outflows related to the company's financing activities, such as borrowing or repayment of debt, or issuing or repurchasing of shares. This section is important as it provides information on the company's capital structure and ability to finance its operations.

Overall, the cash flow statement is an important tool for understanding a company's financial health and cash management practices. By analyzing the statement, investors, creditors, and management can gain insights into the company's ability to generate cash and its financial sustainability.

## REVIEW NET WORTH

Net worth is the value of an individual's assets, minus their liabilities. Assets can include things like cash, investments, real estate, and personal property, while liabilities can include things like mortgages, credit card debt, and other loans. By subtracting one's liabilities from their assets, you can determine their net worth.

Net worth is an important measure of financial health, as it can help individuals understand how much they own and how much they owe. It can also serve as a benchmark for setting financial goals and tracking progress over time. You should compare your Net Worth to previous months to be sure you are not losing net wort in your company. This may mean that your liabilities are creeping up or your revenue is down. You should track down the reason for any significant change from one month to the next.

It's worth noting that net worth can vary widely depending on an individual's income, expenses, investments, and debt. Some people may have a negative net worth if their liabilities exceed their assets, while others may have a positive net worth in the millions or even billions of dollars. Ultimately, net worth is just one measure of financial health, and it's important to consider other factors like income, expenses, and savings when evaluating one's financial situation.

## What other financial data should be reviewed monthly?

In addition to the financial reports already mentioned, there are some others that should be reviewed.

# Profit-izing Your Business

Accounts receivable and payable: Review your accounts receivable (money owed to you by customers) and accounts payable (money you owe to suppliers) to ensure you're managing your cash flow effectively.

Budget vs. actual: Compare your actual expenses and revenue to your budget for the month to identify any areas where you overspent or underspent. This will help you adjust your spending and revenue strategies to stay on track with your business goals.

Sales analysis: Analyze your sales performance for the month, including your best-selling products or services, your most profitable customers, and any trends or patterns in your sales data. This will help you make informed decisions about your marketing and sales strategies.

# Profit-izing Your Business

Tax obligations: Make sure you're up-to-date on your tax obligations and have set aside enough money to cover any upcoming tax payments.

By conducting a monthly financial review that includes these components, small businesses can stay on top of their financial performance and make informed decisions to grow their business.

# Profit-izing Your Business

# CONCLUSION

There has been a lot of information presented in this book. Some of it may be overwhelming for an owner of a small business.

Remember, everything doesn't have to be done at once. Take it one step at a time. Budgeting and making sure your Accounts Receivable and Accounts Payable are under control are three of the most important things you can learn from this book. Once you've dealt with those, the rest should be easy.

# Profit-izing Your Business

# ABOUT THE AUTHOR

Neil Bryan is a successful business consultant. He is a graduate of the University of Redlands in California with both Bachelor's and Master's Degrees in Business Administration.

Along the way he has designed and used paper forms as well as Excel spreadsheets and Access databases to manage and control his business ventures. He is an accomplished systems designer and programmer who designed many specialized business systems including a restaurant management system for a privately owned chain of restaurants, a booking system for a bus tour company and a routing system for a package delivery service.

He has also been involved in many implementations of large-scale computer systems using Oracle Applications, with a specialty in Financials, Procure-to-Pay and Order to Cash systems. His other specialty is Business Process Reengineering, i.e redesigning business processes to streamline them, thereby reducing costs and increasing profit. These projects have taken him throughout the United States with one project in Japan.

Currently he is retired and divides his time with his wife, Maureen, between his summer home in Massachusetts, his winter home in Arizona and traveling the world.

When they aren't traveling, he spends much of his time sorting through his software and forms trying to bring the most practical of these to the general public so others can benefit from them. This book is one of those efforts.

# OTHER BOOKS BY THE AUTHOR

All these books are available at:

**www.amazon.com**

**www.amazon.com/author/neilbryan**

**www.neilbryan.com**

_Quick Reads for Commuters and Others_: Stories, poems, essays, and other writings to read in fifteen minutes or less.

Money Action Plan Series:

1. _Budgeting and Money Management – The Basics:_ A lifelong plan for budgeting and managing your money. This includes free downloadable software.
2. _Keep More of What You Earn_: This book provides all the details of how to review and maximize your

income and how to review and minimize your expenses. It also includes a year's worth of forms for creating a manual budget.

3. _Investing - The Basics_: A step by step investment plan starter plan.

4. _Retirement Planning - The Basics_: Step by step to planning your retirement.

5. _Estate Planning - The Basics_: Step by step to planning your estate.

_Rental Property Records Book:_ Keep all your annual records for up to 12 rental properties in one book.

_Meeting Notes Journal_: For those who still like to jot things down during meetings or conference calls.

# Profit-izing Your Business

_Coursework Notes Journal_: Organize your class and work schedule for academic success!

_The Everyday Planning Book:_ Plan anything you need or want to do.

_Write NOW!:_ Handbook for Organizing, Writing and Formatting your book.

_Write Your First Book in 30 Days:_ This book is about writing a book using the book being written as examples. See the entire process and this book is the finished work.

Neil Bryan Websites:

**www.neimaur.com** - my corporate website with links to all my other sites:

**www.neilbryan.com** - my personal writer's blog

# Profit-izing Your Business

**Mentorship.neilbryan.com** - my Author Mentorship Program

**www.moneyactionplan.com**- the Money Action Plan System

**www.wordstolivewith.com** - ecommerce website

# The End

www.ingramcontent.com/pod-product-compliance
Lightning Source LLC
Chambersburg PA
CBHW070230190526
45169CB00001B/142